MAH-JONGG
from Shanghai to Miami Beach

by Christina Cavallaro *and* Anita Luu

CHRONICLE BOOKS
SAN FRANCISCO

COPYRIGHT © 2005 BY AFFICHE DESIGN, INC. ALL RIGHTS RESERVED.
NO PART OF THIS BOOK MAY BE REPRODUCED IN ANY
FORM WITHOUT WRITTEN PERMISSION FROM THE PUBLISHER.

P. 52: *MAH-JONGG: THE TILES THAT BIND*. MOVIE POSTER
ART BY TIM KIRKMAN © BTG PRODUCTIONS

LIBRARY OF CONGRESS CATALOGING-IN-PUBLICATION DATA AVAILABLE.

ISBN: 0-8118-4733-0

MANUFACTURED IN CHINA

DESIGN BY AFFICHE DESIGN, INC.
PHOTOGRAPHS BY KELLY POWERS.
TYPESET IN ALBERT, CHELTENHAM, AND CLARENDON.

DISTRIBUTED IN CANADA BY RAINCOAST BOOKS
9050 SHAUGHNESSY STREET
VANCOUVER, BRITISH COLUMBIA V6P 6E5

10 9 8 7 6 5 4 3 2 1

CHRONICLE BOOKS LLC
85 SECOND STREET
SAN FRANCISCO, CALIFORNIA 94105

WWW.CHRONICLEBOOKS.COM

To Steve Müller, my huckleberry friend.

~ C.C.

To my grandfather, who introduced me to the game,

and to Sing Lin, who inspires me to keep playing.

~ A.L.

CONTENTS

9

INTRODUCTION

Mah-Jongg: So Old, So New

25

CHAPTER 1

Shanghai to Miami Beach

69

CHAPTER 2

Tiles, Sets, and
Tchotchkes

101

CHAPTER 3

The Traditional Chinese
and American Games

166

RESOURCES

172

ACKNOWLEDGMENTS

174

ABOUT THE AUTHORS

MAH-JONGG: SO OLD, SO NEW

*A journey of a thousand miles must
begin with a single step.*

~ Lao-tzu

CHESS IS STERN, CHECKERS IS A BIT DOTTY, AND SCRABBLE TENDS TO BE WORDY. BUT MAH-JONGG IS SEDUCTIVE. FROM THE RICH LUSTER OF THE TILES AND THE CHALLENGING NATURE OF THE GAME ITSELF TO ITS ENIGMATIC HISTORY AND MAGICAL POWER TO BRING PEOPLE TOGETHER, MAH-JONGG IS NOT JUST A GAME, IT'S A WAY OF LIFE— AND A STYLISH ONE AT THAT. FOR NON-CHINESE-SPEAKING PEOPLE THERE IS SOMETHING THRILLING AND ROMANTIC ABOUT CALLING OUT WORDS LIKE *BAM* AND *CRAK*, *PUNG*, *KONG*, AND *CHOW* DURING PLAY. FOR CHINESE PEOPLE, PLAYING CAN BE A WAY OF CONNECTING WITH A RICH SOCIAL AND CULTURAL HISTORY. AND FOR EVERYONE, IT PROVIDES AN OPPORTUNITY TO BRING TOGETHER A COMMUNITY OF FAMILY AND FRIENDS, AND THE WONDERFUL HOPE OF WIDENING THAT COMMUNITY.

Once upon a time, men and women used to know things—*real* things—like the fox-trot and the Charleston and the tango. Women sewed haute couture as a matter of course and wore gloves and scarves; men made perfect martinis, tied sailing knots, and wore hats. People dressed up when they left the house, and when they came together they played social games such as canasta, bridge, dominoes, chess, Parcheesi, and Go. And mah-jongg. The resurgent popularity of mah-jongg marks, in part, our yearning to return to this sort of stylish, close-knit community. By adding mah-jongg gatherings to their PDAs and diligently sending out e-mail reminders, people today are making mah-jongg an integral part of their social agendas—as regular as going to the gym, as special as going home for the holidays. What more and more people are discovering is that, in an age when long-held rituals and traditions have fallen by the wayside and families and communities have scattered, mah-jongg is the light on the porch—the beacon that calls us home again and reacquaints us with a piece of our past, and each other. The weekly get-togethers, held at a different player's house each week, and the swapping of food and conversation that surround this game fill that gap in our lives. These gatherings are now happening everywhere, from suburban hamlets to retirement communities to hip urban lofts in cities the world over.

Across cultures, ages, and styles of play, the most common thread is the camaraderie and social bonding the game fosters in the spaces between hands. Excluding the play that goes on in serious gambling establishments found mostly in Asia, the game tends to be less about competition and more about community; to a certain extent this is true even among

"MAJONG, THE ANCIENT AND DIVERTING CHINESE GAME" BOX COVER
MADE IN CHINA, BY DESHLER PURCHASING AGENCY, CIRCA 1923

the dedicated cast of regulars on the tournament circuit. Mah-jongg has an almost-otherworldly power to bring people closer, connecting us both to the present and to a past that spans generations.

For newcomers to the game, this possibility of experiencing such a powerful connection is appealing. As one player in California confided, "I have to say, I didn't really like the game at first. I've never really been brilliant at it. For me, it has always been much more about the community, and the intimacy that has formed within my playing circle. We may not necessarily see each other beyond the confines of the game, but the bonds we've formed around the weekly mah-jongg table have seen us through marriages, deaths, love affairs, you name it. Just eight months after joining, it was with this group that I shared my fortieth birthday celebration."

For others, mah-jongg has been part of their lives for almost as long as they can remember. Coauthor Anita Luu, born to Chinese parents in Saigon, Vietnam, recalls how she first came to play the game at the age of four at her grandparents' house in California. "My grandparents always played with my aunts and uncles. And whenever I was visiting and a game was going on, my grandfather would let me sit on his lap. He didn't try to teach me, because I was too young, but I was happy just to watch (and be allowed to sit with the adults). Eventually, he showed me how to play and it drove the other players crazy because he'd hold up the game for me. But now, every time I touch the tiles I think back to those early days of learning on my grandfather's knee, and I am filled with such fond memories and a warm sense of love."

Across cultures and generations, longtime players speak of the game's power to stir cherished memories. A seventy-year-old Northern California woman who plays mah-jongg once a week with her friends confirmed, "When I was growing up in Brooklyn, my mother would have 'the girls' over once a week to play mah-jongg. It was always the same group, and there was always a spread: coffee, cake, raisins, nuts, and candy. They played for years and years. I liked the camaraderie of the group, so she eventually taught me how to play. When I got married, my mother-in-law gave me a beautiful ivory set. Now whenever I play, it brings back lovely memories of both women."

WOMEN PLAYING MAH-JONGG, CIRCA 1923

WHAT'S *in a* NAME?

Mah-jongg—also called *ma jong, mah jong, mah chong, ma jiang, ma que, ma diao, mahjek, ma cheuk, mah cheuck, baak ling, pung chow, ching chow,* and *ning-po*—is one game with many different names, which vary due to region, dialect, licensing and copyright issues, some early attempts at marketing the game, and the transmutation of words that occurs across cultures. The original classical Chinese character for the game was 麻雀 (*ma que*, translated as "hemp sparrow," "jute bird," or "flax bird"). The Cantonese refer to the game as *mahjek*, meaning "sparrow" or "the game of sparrows." The Chinese people consider the sparrow to be an intelligent bird, and mah-jongg, often called "the game of one hundred intelligences," is considered a game for clever people because it can be so challenging. Some also hear the noisy, garbled quality of sparrows' chirps in the distinct sound the tiles make when they're shuffled, and some see a sparrow pecking for food in the way players pick up tiles. Today, in a national effort to simplify the Chinese kanji alphabet, the original character is now written as 麻將 (*ma jiang*, "hemp leader," "jute general," or "flax commander"). However, when the name "Mah Jongg" was patented in 1923 by Joseph P. Babcock, most people around the world began calling it such and still do; most other extrapolations were attempts to avoid copyright infringement claims.

STER
ON
H JONG
H CHEUK
H CHAN
NG CHO

發

SNYDER'S
MA-JUNG
MANUAL

PING-CHOW
IN
TEN MINUTES

平
洲
公
司

Price
Twenty-Five Cents

Foster
FAMOUS RULES
for—
AN-CHU
TRADE MARK

CHING-CHONG
TRADE MARK

Living plants are flexible

In death, they become dry and brittle.

Therefore, stubborn people are disciples of death,

But flexible people are disciples of life.

~ Lao-tzu

ONE GAME, MANY GAMES

Despite the sense of community fostered by the game, the style of play differs from one culture to another. Often people play how their friends play, and styles, rules, setup, and etiquette vary from group to group—often representing the values, customs, and quirks associated with that particular culture or ethnicity. The Japanese for instance—purists by nature—have managed to simplify the rules of mah-jongg without altering the essence of the original Chinese version; while traditional Chinese sets tend toward bright colors and ornate designs, Japanese sets and game play have taken on qualities characteristic of their culture: austerity, minimalism, and tidiness (tile discards are neatly lined up, for example). The American game includes the useful gadget of tile racks, as well as the *Official Standard Hands and Rules* card issued by the National Mah Jongg League.

Because of these differences, and because international tournaments take place everywhere from Tokyo, Japan, to Nijmegen, The Netherlands (host of the Open European Mahjong Championship), chat rooms are filled with people asking and answering questions related to setup and rules of the game. Tournament organizers are always seeking ways to accommodate the myriad styles amongst the various cultural groups who come to compete.

Organizers of the first-ever World Championship in Mahjong, held in Tokyo in 2002, estimate that close to 5 million people, in countries all over the world (including Asia, Europe, South Africa, Canada, and the United States), play mah-jongg. Given the game's widespread popularity, the Tokyo tournament organizers have said that they hope to one day bring mah-jongg to the Olympics. Reflecting the unifying spirit of the Olympic games, mah-jongg, many feel, would be a natural addition to the roster. Unlike other global games such as Ping-Pong and chess, which come with essentially universal rules, mah-jongg requires a certain amount of cooperation, diplomacy, and consensus before participants can even begin to engage in play. If the United Nations were to ever select an official game to best represent their body, mah-jongg would be the perfect fit.

MAH JONGG SCORE CARD, NEW YORK, CIRCA 1923

For many younger players it is this multicultural aspect that draws them, and it provides as much intrigue and interest as the game itself. Students from all over the world are bridging cultural gaps through university-organized mah-jongg tournaments and exchanges, wherein Midwestern athletes sit across from Southeast Asian engineers, and young Japanese women "chow," "pung," and whip the pants off Dutch opponents.

For collectors, designers, and lovers of chinoiserie, Bakelite, and mid-twentieth-century design, the game also offers a striking aesthetic richness. Today's artists, inspired by the natural beauty of the tiles, are finding creative ways to add a dash of mah-jongg flair to everything from modern floor lamps and furniture to elegant earrings, pendants, cuff links, and hip chunky bracelets worn by fashionistas and Hollywood celebrities.

Full of nostalgia and style, with the appeal of a book group and the glamour of a cotillion ball, mah-jongg is the social butterfly of the game world—beautiful, smart, sophisticated, and well traveled, with a very active social life and the dazzling power to bring people of all kinds together.

MA CHEUCK GAME BOX, BY THE HILLSON COMPANY, BOSTON, CIRCA 1923

CHAPTER 1 ◉ SHANGHAI TO MIAMI BEACH

Study the past if you would divine the future.

~ Confucius

THE WONDER YEARS

AS BEFITS ANY RICHLY STORIED AND BELOVED CULTURAL PHENOMENON, MAH-JONGG CARRIES WITH IT A COLORFUL ARRAY OF TALES AND LEGENDS TO ACCOUNT FOR ITS ORIGINS. ONE PARTICULARLY FAR-FETCHED, BUT NONETHE-LESS OFT-TOLD, THEORY HAS IT THAT THE GAME WAS PLAYED AS EARLY AS 2350 B.C. ABOARD NOAH'S ARK DURING THE FORTY LONG DAYS AND NIGHTS OF RAIN. ACCORDING TO THE STORY, THE WIND, WHICH BLEW FROM THE EAST DURING THE STORM, LED THESE EARLY PLAYERS TO DESIGNATE THE EASTERN SEATING POSITION THE DOMINANT ONE IN THE GAME.

STILL ANOTHER STORY, ALAS PROBABLY ALSO A ROMANTIC MYTH, PINS THE ORIGIN ON THE GREAT CHINESE PHILOSOPHER CONFUCIUS, CLAIMING HE DEVELOPED THE GAME AROUND 500 B.C. AS A SORT OF VISUAL AID FOR USE IN THE TEACHING OF HIS DOCTRINE.

WIZARDS FROM CHINESE FOLKLORE PLAYING MAH-JONGG, UNDATED

The three dragon tiles (red, green, and white), known as "honor tiles," and their attached symbolic meanings do actually coincide with the three cardinal virtues taught by Confucius at the time: Benevolence, Sincerity, and Filial Piety. And Confucius loved birds, which neatly ties to the game's Chinese name, the word for "sparrow."

However (no offense to Confucius), the most logical line of thinking suggests that the game was derived from the various Chinese tile and card games, originally played by peasants, that have been around in one form or another since about A.D. 1120. One such game is the domino-esque *kap tai shap.* In this game, as in mah-jongg, a wall is built, dice are cast, and tiles are drawn. However, although it is true that kap tai shap and other domino-like games have long been played fervently by the Chinese people, mah-jongg actually bears a stronger resemblance to certain card games similar in structure to gin rummy. One such game, *ya pei,* thought to have been played during the Sung Dynasty (A.D. 960–1279), employed thirty-two cards marked with numbers one through nine, and featured four flowers per deck, elements that remain a part of the game of mah-jongg today. These early cards were made of either wood or ivory and had an oblong shape similar to that of a mah-jongg tile.

A new game, *matiao,* which came into vogue during the Ming Dynasty (A.D. 1368–1644) and found favor among peasants, featured forty paper cards, similar to the ones used in ya pei. These cards numbered one through nine in four different suits and included four different flower cards. Matiao was a gambling game for four players, played with four

MATIAO PLAYING CARDS, MADE IN CHINA, CIRCA 1900

cards bearing suits pertaining to money. Three of the four matiao suits resembled the three suits of mah-jongg: coins corresponded to dots, strings of coins corresponded to bams, and groupings of strings of coins corresponded to craks. Matiao is similar enough to mah-jongg to be considered by most historians as its closest antecedent.

It's unclear why matiao cards were made of paper while other game cards were made of ivory or bamboo, but it likely relates to the fact that these and other gambling pursuits were (and still are) illegal in China. It was decidedly cheaper and more practical to use paper cards, which could be quickly cast into a fire or thrown away if players were suddenly

CONFUCIUS
on
MAH-JONGG

Even if you don't accept the theory that Confucius created the game, you will perhaps do well to heed his sage advice in play as in other matters.

THE MAN WHO STANDS ON HILL WITH MOUTH OPEN WILL WAIT LONG TIME FOR ROAST DUCK TO DROP IN.

LEARNING WITHOUT THOUGHT IS LABOR LOST; THOUGHT WITHOUT LEARNING IS PERILOUS.

HUMILITY IS THE SOLID FOUNDATION OF ALL VIRTU

THOSE WHO DO NOT STUDY ARE ONLY CATTLE DRESSED UP IN MEN'S CLOTHES.

THE CAUTIOUS SELDOM ERR.

SUCCESS DEPENDS UPON PREVIOUS PREPARATION, AND WITHOUT SUCH PREPARATION THERE IS SURE TO BE FAILURE.

IF YOU SHOOT FOR THE STARS AND HIT THE MOON, IT IS ACCEPTABLE.

in danger of being caught by authorities. But in 1850, around the time of the Tai Ping Rebellion, a high-ranking officer in the city of Ningbo, Zheijiang Province, by the name of Chen Yumen, decided to revive the use of matiao tiles, which had fallen out of favor. He began commissioning artisans to transpose the designs from the flimsy, lightweight cards onto the sturdier, more permanent tiles, only this time with more elegance. Chen Yumen, in his desire to make the game more appealing for play among friends, is credited with starting what would become known as the game of mah-jongg.

This early form of the game, using tiles, soon became an exclusive pastime of the aristocracy, due to Chen Yumen's class and wealth; he would have played the game with his moneyed peers, who could have afforded the cost of hand-carved, painted sets made of the finest materials, while peasants clearly could not. Since the wealthy had their sets custom made, many incorporated court symbols and characters relating to Chinese numerology, which was (and remains today) an important element of Chinese culture. And because of its charm and aesthetic appeal, mah-jongg grew to be so much more than just a game—it became intertwined with people's lives, identities, and even their divination practices. Though both the tile and card versions of matiao migrated across the country over the fifteen years that followed, replacing chess as the most popular game in China, the cards eventually disappeared in favor of the tiles—which became popular even among the masses once they became affordable.

With the rules of the game still being loosely interpreted, there was definitely room for some streamlining, and soon a whole host of very specific setup rituals were being used, leading to the pomp and circumstance we recognize in the game today. Though the careful shuffling and building of the four walls into a perfect square and the almost-compulsive, precise splitting of the wall might appear to be a nonessential dog-and-pony show to the newcomer, these elements were originally incorporated to prevent cheating—after all, mah-jongg by origin is no stranger to gambling.

In 1911, when the ruling class fell and the Republic came to be, the game migrated to illegal gambling parlors, where only men were allowed to engage in play. Eventually it spread to the general public, becoming popular predominantly among women, who played the game at home and also enjoyed gambling, but were careful not to openly discuss their illegal activities. The game provided a primary social outlet for many women during an era when most did not have careers beyond the domestic front and men were often away working. Asian women still play together on a regular basis, with some exchange of money involved, but for the most part the game is regarded as more of a social activity, as portrayed in Amy Tan's novel and the subsequent film *The Joy Luck Club*, in which lifelong friendships among four women evolve and revolve around the game of mah-jongg.

During the decade of the Cultural Revolution (1966–76), China's government, ruled by Mao Zedong, cracked down harder than ever before on drinking and gambling of any kind. The clicking of tiles, once commonly heard at events such as wedding receptions and banquets, was effectively silenced. Anybody daring to disobey the laws of the time was dealt harsh punishment, and fear of reprisals forced the game underground, where it was still played, but much more quietly. It wasn't until after the Cultural Revolution ended with the death of Chairman Mao in 1976 that mah-jongg slowly came back into fashion as a national pastime, embraced by young couples and families who knew the place it had held in their grandparents' and great-grandparents' lives.

Perhaps because the game first became popular with the masses in Asian social clubs and gambling parlors, the mah-jongg played in Asia and in Asian communities in the United States and Canada is still closely associated with serious gambling, primarily among men. In these communities, scoring can be complicated, and sizeable losses are a regular occurrence. Gambling related to the game is notoriously rife in Japan, where many businessmen consider a stop at a mah-jongg arcade on the way home from work to be de rigueur, as common as an after-work cocktail. In China, however, the gambling element is simultaneously rampant and hush-hush. According to mah-jongg historian Tom Sloper, in 1988 a sports-related ministry of the Chinese government, acknowledging the existence of gambling in mah-jongg in a country that legally forbids such activity, established a set of tournament rules for the game. The rules set up a structure wherein participants would play for points, rather than money, in observance of the law. Although most people outside of the tournament circuit in China still play for money in their own homes and in clubs and gaming establishments, they are simply more discreet when it becomes time to settle up.

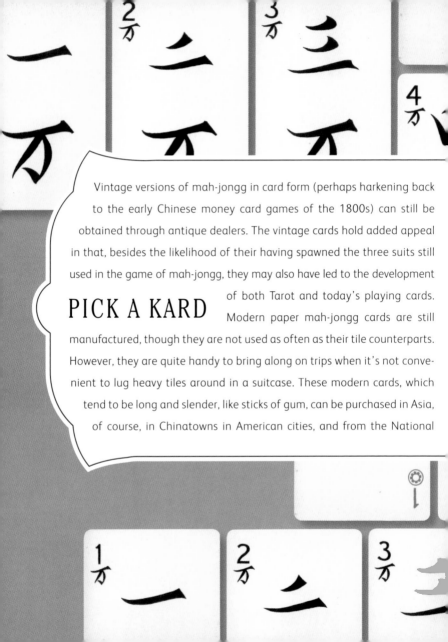

Vintage versions of mah-jongg in card form (perhaps harkening back to the early Chinese money card games of the 1800s) can still be obtained through antique dealers. The vintage cards hold added appeal in that, besides the likelihood of their having spawned the three suits still used in the game of mah-jongg, they may also have led to the development of both Tarot and today's playing cards.

PICK A KARD

Modern paper mah-jongg cards are still manufactured, though they are not used as often as their tile counterparts. However, they are quite handy to bring along on trips when it's not convenient to lug heavy tiles around in a suitcase. These modern cards, which tend to be long and slender, like sticks of gum, can be purchased in Asia, of course, in Chinatowns in American cities, and from the National

Mah Jongg League in the United States. (The latter are called "kards," a holdover from a boom time in the game's U.S. popularity when variations of the game were patented to discourage commercial competition. Play with paper cards is much the same as with the tile version, but with minor adjustments; for example, building a wall is not necessary when you can simply stack all the cards, one on top of the other.)

These days, on warm summer nights in Shanghai, the clicking of tiles can be heard once more, floating out through open windows into the streets. The game is now once again played in full force in banquet halls and at wedding receptions across China. Where in other cultures guests might push aside the tables in order to do the limbo or the conga, Chinese people set the tables up right in the middle of the room and ring in the happy occasion with rousing games of mah-jongg. Chinese people also like to play mah-jongg on days that are considered lucky: the day a child is born is often marked by a party and mah-jongg session, and New Year's celebrations include the game as well.

MAH-JONGG IN AMERICA AND BEYOND

Mah-jongg is thought to have been introduced to the Western world in the early 1900s by two brothers named White, who brought it to the English clubs in Shanghai. The game quickly gained popularity among foreign residents there. Its inherent elegance, beauty, and built-in excuse for socializing also spoke to the ebullient soul and decadence of the flapper era. Consequently, mah-jongg hit it big in the 1920s, quickly becoming the favored pastime among the rich and stylish in Japan, Europe, India, and the United States.

Savvy American businessman Joseph P. Babcock, then the Soochow city representative of the Standard Oil Company, saw the popularity of the game among foreigners in Shanghai and quickly recognized a business

"PUNG WO–JUNIOR" BOX COVER, CIRCA 1920

PUNG WO=JUNIOR

(TRADE MARK)

THE ROYAL GAME OF CHINA

PLAYED FOR THOUSANDS OF
YEARS IN THE LAND OF CONFUCIUS

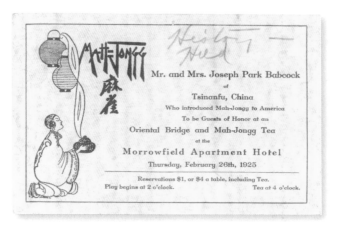

INVITATION TO MRS. JOSEPH BABCOCK'S MAH-JONGG PARTY, 1925

opportunity ripe for the picking. He imported the first sets into the United States, and in September 1920, in an effort to ensure their commercial success, he copyrighted and put into print for the first time a set of substantially simplified, no-frills rules: *Babcock's Rules for Mah-Jongg: The Red Book of Rules*. He is also credited with starting the practice of having English numerals carved above the kanji characters on the tiles, initially contracting Chinese craftsmen to do the job. A few years later, in 1923, he returned to the States and patented the name "Mah-Jongg." It was his slogan that eventually made its way onto all sets manufactured in and exported from China by what would become the Mah-Jongg Sales Company of America: "If it isn't marked 'Mah-Jongg' it isn't genuine."

MRS. JOSEPH BABCOCK (CENTER) WITH HER MAH-JONGG FRIENDS, CIRCA 1924

In America the game was met with a fervor befitting the roaring twenties and captivated people on both coasts with its exoticism. In the beginning, only the wealthiest Americans tended to play, using pricey imported sets of hand-carved ivory and bamboo. Two years later, W. A. Hammond, a lumber merchant from San Francisco working in conjunction with Babcock, formed the Mah-Jongg Sales Company of San Francisco (which eventually became the Mah-Jongg Sales Company of America) and began the commercial importation of less expensive Chinese-manufactured mah-jongg sets, made of bone. The lower prices allowed more people to afford the sets. In September 1922 the San Francisco Chamber of Commerce reported that mah-jongg sets valued at a total of $56,000 had been shipped from Shanghai up to that time, and that most of these had been shipped by Hammond's company.

The year 1923 marked the height of mah-jongg's popularity in the United States. Mah-jongg sets numbered sixth in exports from Shanghai, generating revenues of more than $1.5 million that year alone. To enable the Chinese manufacturers to meet the overwhelming demand for mah-jongg

sets, the shinbones of cattle were shipped from the United States to Shanghai. It was at this time that a number of American-based companies also began stateside production of sets, including Parker Brothers, United States Playing Card, and Milton Bradley—the latter of which was saved from bankruptcy when its factories began churning out mah-jongg sets around the clock in order to keep up with consumer demand. Parker Brothers, like many game manufacturers of the time, included a copy of *Babcock's Rules for Mah-Jongg* in every one of their sets, evidence of a licensing agreement between the game company and Babcock for its use of his patented name, "Mah-Jongg."

Pretty soon everyone in the business wanted a piece of the action, and mah-jongg merchants, importers, and retailers began offering demos and lessons to attract new players—and new dollars—to the game. Enterprising businessmen set up game tables on street corners and in storefront windows to create a buzz and teach people how to play. In an effort to capitalize on its popularity, even businesses that had no connection to the game began giving out free scorecards, rulebooks, and all manner of

mah-jongg items branded with their company logos. At the height of its success, it was the most popular game in America.

By the end of 1923 people all over the country had become so skilled at the game that they were outgrowing the "student driver" version of the rules created by Joseph Babcock. To increase the challenge, players started making up their own rules, adding new twists and "special hands."

STANDARDIZATION COMMITTEE OF THE
AMERICAN OFFICIAL LAWS OF MAH-JONGG, 1924

Country clubs, hotels, steamship lines, and mah-jongg parlors, now cropping up everywhere, all published their own sets of house rules. These new, individualized rules led to many fun variations, but also to much confusion.

In 1924, several mah-jongg rule-book authors (M. C. Work, Robert Foster, Joseph Babcock, Lee Hartman, and J. H. Smith) formed a standardization committee in order to bring a consistent structure back to the game. Their collaboration led to the publication of *The American Official Laws of Mah-Jongg*. However, their efforts were for naught. Unfortunately, mah-jongg instructors in clubs continued to incorporate their own rules and strategies, and various new leagues and organizations promoted still more rules, all of which led to the fragmentation and dilution of the original game. As a result, the potency of the game, and Americans' passion for it, dissolved.

However, only a few years later, a couple of factors laid the foundation for the game's rebirth. Mah-jongg got its groove back when two new organizations formed to give it wings. First, the wives of servicemen stationed at Wright-Patterson Air Force Base in McCook Field, Ohio, established a league around 1930 using their own set of rules and hands so that, no matter where their country called them, they could continue to play with a standardized set of rules at bases worldwide. The Wright-Patterson rules were officially published and copyrighted in 1963 and are still in use today. (A league associated with the U.S. Navy established its own set of rules as well.) Second, the National Mah Jongg League was formed in New York City in 1937 when another group of interested

players created a standard set of rules in an effort to bring the game back into the mainstream. This time it stuck. Still thriving today, the National Mah Jongg League boasts a membership of more than 250,000 players; publishes instruction books, newsletters, and the annual *Official Standard Hands and Rules* card; and organizes tournaments and other events.

Some of the founders of the league, and many of its longstanding members, were Jewish. Throughout World War II the game continued to be played among Jewish women's circles as it increased in popularity and became more prevalent in their lives. Then and now, the league contributes a portion of its earnings to numerous charities, with upwards of $600,000 per year going to a variety of Jewish and other causes.

One possible explanation for the game's popularity in Jewish communities is that Jews fleeing the Nazis and settling in Shanghai might have picked up the game there before moving to the United States after World War II. Shanghai was one of the very few places that did not require an entry visa during the war, so Jews who could not find another country to accept them fled across Russia, down through Japan, and into Shanghai to escape the Nazis. Displaced from their homeland, they involved themselves to some extent in the local Chinese culture, which included learning mah-jongg. Postwar diaspora from Shanghai may have had a hand in bringing the game to the Jewish communities of the midwestern, northeastern, and southeastern United States.

U.S. MAH-JONGG STORE DISPLAY, CIRCA 1923

Whatever the cause, even before the influx of Jews from Shanghai, mah-jongg found a devoted audience in the close-knit urban Jewish American communities, especially among women. It's easy to see why: in a depressed economy, with most men off to war, mah-jongg was a fun, cheap, and communal form of entertainment. Neighbors, friends, mothers, and daughters taught one another with zeal, helping to revive a game that for the previous ten years had been quietly sleeping. When the men returned (favoring poker for their social activity), many women adopted bridge, canasta, pinochle, knitting, and other activities, but in Jewish communities mah-jongg remained the women's game of choice—it was back and here to stay.

[Seeking] Mah Jong partners for mother-in-law.

~ Craigslist.org posting from Miami, Florida

MIAMI BEACH CONNECTION

Although mah-jongg players in the over-fifty-five crowd are still predominantly female, the demographic is much more diverse now than it used to be, according to National Mah-Jongg League president Ruth Unger. She attributes this changing cultural demographic to the increased popularity of leisure groups of all kinds, from classic car clubs to wine appreciation circles to hiking organizations, reaching across cultures, ages, and nationalities. However, although the game is played in large numbers in New York and surrounding areas, as well as in Florida, Arizona, California, Maryland, and New Jersey, not surprisingly there is a notoriously strong mah-jongg presence among retirees in the Miami Beach area, a major retirement destination for East Coast residents, many of them Jewish.

The actual learning of the game has often been described as a near rite of passage among Jewish women. But according to Unger, during the 1950s and 1960s the game lost popularity among young women as feminism came to the fore. "Women didn't want to play a game they thought was a frivolous thing their mothers played. They wanted to do great things with their lives…. I don't care who you are, or where you're from, nobody wants to be like their mother." However, the game is persistent and seductive, and poetic justice is usually served when the daughter who has strayed ends up liking it far more than her mother ever did. These prodigal daughters came to realize that the intangible element of the game—its power to hold their mother's circle of friends together in support and friendship—was not frivolous at all, Unger says.

Unger further asserts that as mah-jongg gets passed on from one group to another it has a mushroom effect. This is very much in keeping with the tradition of the league itself, she says, which has never used major public promotion or advertising or tried to drum up business. Membership and interest in the game come about mostly through word of mouth. The game has been propagated in a similar manner in retirement communities like the ones in the Miami Beach area. Most people end up teaching one person, or two or three, so they have a group to play with, and then those people teach two friends, and so on. At a time of life not often associated with the making of new friends, mah-jongg is at the head of the social committee, around which initiates are happy to gather.

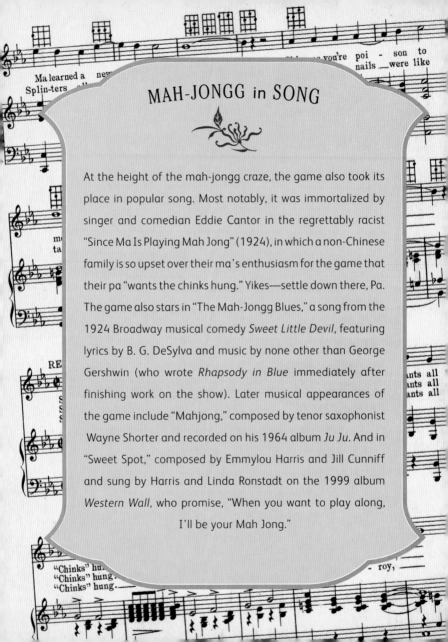

MAH-JONGG in SONG

At the height of the mah-jongg craze, the game also took its place in popular song. Most notably, it was immortalized by singer and comedian Eddie Cantor in the regrettably racist "Since Ma Is Playing Mah Jong" (1924), in which a non-Chinese family is so upset over their ma's enthusiasm for the game that their pa "wants the chinks hung." Yikes—settle down there, Pa. The game also stars in "The Mah-Jongg Blues," a song from the 1924 Broadway musical comedy *Sweet Little Devil*, featuring lyrics by B. G. DeSylva and music by none other than George Gershwin (who wrote *Rhapsody in Blue* immediately after finishing work on the show). Later musical appearances of the game include "Mahjong," composed by tenor saxophonist Wayne Shorter and recorded on his 1964 album *Ju Ju*. And in "Sweet Spot," composed by Emmylou Harris and Jill Cunniff and sung by Harris and Linda Ronstadt on the 1999 album *Western Wall*, who promise, "When you want to play along, I'll be your Mah Jong."

SINCE MA IS PLAYING
MAH JONG

Ukulele Accompaniment

Sung with great Success
By **EDDIE**
CANTOR
in **KID BOOTS**
Direction FLORENZ ZIEGFELD

BILLY ROSE and
ON CONRAD

M. Witmark & Sons

TILES ARE A GIRL'S BEST FRIEND

Mah-jongg has been making its way into the lives of the hip and stylish, too—and into the pages of their magazines. Readers wrote letters by the bagful to the "Where Can I Find . . ." section of *InStyle* magazine when Julia Roberts was spotted on-screen wearing a chic chinoiserie-inspired bracelet of sandalwood, Chinese coral beads, and antique mah-jongg tiles. And if a simple strand worn around the wrist isn't enough to sate the fashion hungry, there's mah-jongg-inspired designer furniture to be had, like the floor lamp, forty-seven tiles high from base to shade, that was pictured in one *Home and Garden*. A *New York Times Magazine* article titled "We Got Games," commenting on the modern popularity of mah-jongg and other games, said: "The low-tech pastime is back."

MAH-JONGG: THE TILES THAT BIND
MOVIE POSTER, 1989

A *New York Times* article by trend-spotting journalist Susan Campos about Los Angeles movers and shakers who play mah-jongg together bears further witness to the resurgence in the popularity of the game, and to a whole new demographic of players. According to the article, once a week in a Beverly Hills home, a group of agents, entertainment execs, and wives of Hollywood moguls gather together to eat, play mah-jongg, and perhaps network—the latter only if it doesn't interfere with the game. And, offering proof that things

Ma Chiang Matinees

Mrs. Prescott Warren

Is resuming her matinees for both beginners and advanced players, at her Ma Chiang Studio

281 DARTMOUTH ST., BOSTON

(IN THE HELEN CROSBY BUILDING)

FEB. 19 AND 26, MAR. 4 AND 11

From 2.30 to 5 Mrs. Warren will teach and interpret the new Laws of the Standardization Committee (of which she is a member) of the International Ma Chiang Players' Association, and will supervise and instruct at the tables.

The fee is $1.50 for each Matinee, or $5 for the series. Tickets are transferable. Mrs. Warren will also be at her Studio Tuesdays and Thursdays for private and class instruction in Ma Chiang and Auction.

Communications will have prompt attention if addressed to Mrs. Prescott Warren. **35 Hyde Ave., Newton, Mass., Tel. Newton North 0088.**

MAH-JONGG

Instruction by pupil of "Mr. Joseph Park Babcock," of Shanghai who adapted all that was best of the various Chinese forms of play evolved and introduced the game of Mah-Jong.

Appointments may be made by telephone Brookline 7032.

Specially selected Mah-Jongg sets for sale. Also Babcock's complete rules. Address P.G.B., Transcript: Boston 8.

KNOWN IN CHINA AS

MAH-JONG

SPECIAL SET 144 nicely finished wooden tiles, 115 scores, 8 pages of rules, a beautiful set of Ebony finished dice and a racks

RACKS—Beautiful Ebony finished, $4.25

Mail orders promptly filled, postage 15c extra. $1.50 per set

PAULS SPECIALTY SHOP

335 Mass. Ave., Near Huntington Ave., Boston

Mrs. C. L. Grammer Teacher of MA CHIANG

Member of International Ma Chiang Players' Association. HOTEL KEMPTON, Boston, Mass., 831:

NEWSPAPER CLIPPINGS, CIRCA 1923

have come full circle, one interviewee in *The Tiles That Bind*, a fascinating and quirky documentary by Phyllis Heller and Bari Pearlman, puts the trend into perspective: "For many folks from the war era, all their circles of friends played. It was very social. First it was at one person's house, then at another's. It was just part of life, like going out to eat—people just did it." And it seems that people are just doing it again.

The aesthetics of the tiles themselves, with their ancient feel and lustrous color, are just one of the draws for a new generation of players. The romance of the game's history and the collectibility of old sets, found online and in flea markets and antique stores, is also alluring. Many have become familiar with the game by way of their computers and the tile-matching-game sites populating the Internet. And still others have memories of their own grandmothers' love for the game and hope to establish similar traditions in their own lives.

MAH-JONGG
or not
MAH-JONGG?

Though the popular, intricate tile-matching games found on the Internet have helped to bring new devotees to the game of mah-jongg, these games are in fact *not* mah-jongg, even though they are often referred to as such. Video-game designer, producer, and mah-jongg historian Tom Sloper, who designed the *Shanghai: Second Dynasty* game collection for Activision, said, "Many fans of tile-matching games think they are playing mah-jongg, but no. Although the tile-matching games are undeniably fun, and very helpful for training beginners to spot tiles among a plethora of other tiles, tile matching is not mah-jongg." Sometimes called "mah-jongg

solitaire," tile matching involves tiles that are stacked up on-screen in distinct pyramid-like formations, from which players must match and remove tiles from the stacks. Sloper encourages players to think of tile matching, metaphorically, as solitaire, and the game of mah-jongg as gin rummy—two different games played with the same set of cards.

While working at Activision, Sloper was asked to come up with new tile-matching games every few years, and he took the opportunity to create something that more closely resembled the real game of mah-jongg. In order to do this, he proceeded to become an expert in the classical Chinese style of play and most everything else related to mah-jongg. His Web site, www.sloperama.com, is not only a destination for video-game buffs but also a testament to his vast knowledge of the game.

"I was thrown out of N.Y.U. my freshman year for cheating on my metaphysics final, you know. I looked within the soul of the boy sitting next to me. When I was thrown out, my mother, who was an emotionally high-strung woman, locked herself in the bathroom and took an overdose of mah-jongg tiles."

~ Woody Allen (as comedian Alvy Singer in Annie Hall)

CRUISE SHIPS AND TOURNAMENTS AND VEGAS—OH, MY

The rise of international enthusiasm for the game was marked by the 2002 World Championship in Mahjong, the first of its kind, held in Tokyo, Japan. Over an intense two-day period, players from China, Taiwan, Southeast Asia, Japan, Holland, Russia, Sweden, and the United States competed for team and individual trophies (but not money, since international tournaments held in Asia and Europe adhere to the Chinese rules established in 1998, which forbid competition for cash) at the Hotel Grand Palace. This tournament paved the way for the follow-up China Majiang Championship in 2003, held in the city of Hainan, where again players from all over the world met to share in their love for the game. In 2004 the Chinese Majiang Championship Organizing Committee followed up the successful tournament with another, now annual, competition, this one held in Hong Kong. The Dutch hosted the Open European Mahjong Championship in 2004.

In addition to these international tournaments, dozens of large and small competitions are held across the United States, with several agencies orchestrating multiple tournaments each. Roberta and Steve Last of Travel Wizard, a travel agency of more than ten years in La Mesa, California, co-organize the Marjorie Troum tournaments in Las Vegas and Palm Springs each year, together with director and tournament namesake Troum (whose mother, Dorothy Myerson, was one of the National Mah Jongg League's original members, helping to standardize the rules in 1937). These tournaments, generally three days long, are held at luxury hotels where wives will often participate in the mah-jongg competitions during the day while their husbands play golf together at nearby courses. There is generally a mah-jongg mini-tournament held on Saturday nights, except at Vegas tournaments, which are held mostly during the week and never include scheduled nighttime games—because, according to Mr. Last, everybody wants to go out and hit the strip. The Lasts are also known for their Cruise, Schmooze, and Mahj tournaments at sea that take players to such places as Mexico, Alaska, Hawaii, the Caribbean, Canada, New England,

SCORE METERS, CIRCA 1924

HAND-CARVED BONE
COUNTING STICKS USED
FOR SCORE KEEPING, CIRCA 1920

Europe, and the Panama Canal. These mah-jongg tournaments and cruises in the United States are most popular with the fifty-five-and-older set; however, lots of families will use them as a chance to not only play mah-jongg but also to reunite with far-flung sisters, brothers, daughters, sons, cousins, and grandkids for some vacation time. Whether they're held in Las Vegas casinos, in high-rise hotels in Palm Springs, or on cruise ships in the Caribbean, these mah-jongg events and excursions have helped fuel the game's renewed popularity.

The tournament schedules themselves can be somewhat grueling and may in part account for the scarcity of younger, less-experienced players on the circuit. Mah-jongg tournaments are marathons of play and are no place for the fainthearted. Building up endurance over a lifetime of play is the only way one could hold up during the sometimes fifteen-hour days. A veteran tournament participant may average as many as four weekly games of up to twelve hours a session, plus time spent on the Internet in games against opponents all over the world—the equivalent of a full-time job.

In general alcohol is not served at these organized events, and the tournaments are all about good, clean fun (except for the jokes, which can get pretty randy). Travel Wizard tournaments are renowned for their complimentary licorice, *always* red, as well as the popular build-your-own-ice-cream-sundae nights. Even in Las Vegas—Sin City—players tend to favor thinking over drinking, keeping their eyes instead on the $500 grand prize and trophy, which

"PA AND MA JONGG" *LIFE* **MAGAZINE COVER,** APRIL 24, 1924, ISSUE

Life

 PA AND MA JONGG

depicts an angel victoriously holding aloft a mah-jongg tile. But most in the close-knit circle of tournament and cruise participants will admit that they're in it more for the camaraderie than the competition.

Travel Wizard isn't the only agency in the business of organizing mah-jongg tournaments. They share the stage with rival organizer Mah-Jongg Madness, based in Sarasota, Florida, and run by Dorothy and Larry Krams, who started the business more than twenty years ago, when Larry Krams's now ninety-year-old mother, a lifelong mah-jongg devotee, suggested they contact the National Mah Jongg League about setting up an annual tournament for members. Mah-Jongg Madness now holds an average of eight tournaments a year in cities including Deerfield, Illinois; Atlantic City; Boca Raton; Fort Lauderdale; and Las Vegas. The largest land tournament they host is held in Las Vegas, a three-day affair (most of their others last two days) comprising up to 550 participants. Dorothy Krams points out that Mah-Jongg Madness strictly adheres to the National Mah Jongg League rules, and they run a tight ship in other ways, too. Their tournaments are entirely computerized to keep track of players' points throughout competition, leading to a cumulative pot for winners of sometimes close to $2,000, depending on attendance numbers. All tables are a uniform thirty by thirty inches and all sets are provided by Mah-Jongg Madness to ensure perfect tiles; absolutely no outside sets are allowed. In addition to these tournaments, the Kramses organize the annual weeklong cruise for the National Mah Jongg League, which sails the Caribbean and has a sizeable waiting list, given its maximum occupancy of just three hundred passengers.

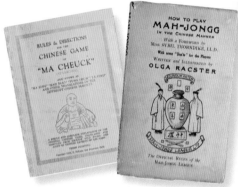

Formed in 1999, a relative newbie on the tournament scene is the American Mah-Jongg Association (AMJA), which hosts an average of four yearly land tournaments plus their own eleven-day Caribbean cruise (offering play from daybreak to dusk to those who want it). The AMJA identifies itself as the "mah-jongg association for the new millennium," representing all forms of the game, including those played on the Internet and all over the world, unlike other organizations that focus on particular versions of the game. Because of this broader representation, AMJA welcomes both the recently initiated and the veteran alike. Correspondingly, the average age of participants in AMJA tournaments seems to be slightly younger than that of participants in tournaments run by other organizations.

Beyond cruise-ship outings and highly orchestrated, trophy-festooned, cash-prize events, there are also a few smaller-scale charity-driven monthly tournaments, many of which take place in and around the Miami Beach area. One such event, started in West Palm Beach by veteran organizer

MAH-JONGG BOOKS, CIRCA 1920

Dorothy Kornheiser, was established to raise money for the group's charity of choice, Hadassa. The participants are experienced players who play at least once a week in other groups, but once a month get together and raise a heap of money for charity. Though Kornheiser has since moved to another Florida community, the West Palm Beach tournament she set in motion is still going strong, as are similar charity tournaments across the country. The possibility of helping others by playing mah-jongg is a very meaningful aspect of the game for these players.

And so, while the hokey I ♥ mah-jongg mugs, T-shirts, bumper stickers, license plate frames, and key chains favored by these tournament-goers might draw wry smiles from today's trendier mah-jongg devotees, who prefer to adorn themselves in chic bangles of Bakelite, it cannot be denied that there is much love surrounding the game for this particular group of diehard fans, who are not afraid to wear it on their sleeves, mugs, or the backs of their cars.

Better a diamond with a flaw
than a pebble without.

~ Confucius

TICKLING THE IVORY, BAMBOO, BAKELITE, BONE, BOXWOOD . . .

THERE IS A SENSUAL, APPEALING ASPECT TO THE GAME OF MAH-JONGG THAT HAS MUCH TO DO WITH THE TACTILE ELEMENT OF PLAY. THE TILES ARE COOL AND SLIGHTLY CREAMY, LIKE THE LACQUERED SURFACE OF A TOFFEE, AND AS SMOOTH AS PIANO KEYS (WHICH LEADS SOME PLAYERS TO ADD A SIGNATURE JERRY LEE LEWIS–TYPE FLOURISH TO THE SETUP OF THEIR WALL, RUNNING A FINGER UP AND DOWN THE LINE OF TILES AS IF IT WERE A KEYBOARD). THE CHINESE HAVE DESCRIBED THE SOUND OF THE TILES AS THAT OF "CLATTERING SPARROWS" WHEN THEY ARE SHUFFLED, OR "WASHED," AS IT IS CALLED WHEN THE PIECES ARE SWIRLED AROUND THE TABLE BY DIFFERENT PAIRS OF HANDS. IT'S A BEAUTIFULLY EVOCATIVE SOUND, A TIMELESS ECHOING FROM THE PAST, LIKE THE IVORY BEADS OF AN ABACUS BEING CLICKED TOGETHER.

HAND-CARVED BONE MAH-JONGG SET, FROM CHINA, QING DYNASTY

HAND-CARVED IVORY FLOWER AND SEASON TILES, CIRCA 1960

The hypnotic sound of the washing of the tiles can be quite soothing; many Asian mothers who play the game during pregnancy say that once the baby is born the best way to calm the child is with the rhythmic clicking sound of mah-jongg tiles.

It's appropriate that the tiles resemble keys on a piano, because, like musicians who become familiar with their instrument, the weight and feel of it, mah-jongg players too become accustomed to their tiles. Just as a different instrument would momentarily feel strange to the musician and take some getting used to, the same is true of mah-jongg tiles. One becomes intimately acquainted with the size, weight, and feel of the particular tiles in one's hand; the material from which they are made; the intricacy of the designs on the tile faces; and even the color. And once you've grown accustomed to a set, it can be either a pleasure or a disappointment to be introduced to something new.

Vintage sets, while beautiful and rich with history, can also present difficulties in play. The chance to play with an inherited set of some age can make beginners feel a little giddy after having played with a modern game manufacturer's standard-issue package—until they are confronted with the new and unfamiliar images on the tiles. In addition to the learning curve that goes along with starting to play with a vintage set (or any unfamiliar set), there may be other difficulties to contend with, such as the warping of antique tiles due to age, which can make them difficult to stack while building the wall and can lead to the occasional tumble and inadvertently revealed tile. The natural curve of bamboo makes for a gorgeous tile in a vintage set, but it can be challenging to play with, especially for beginners, when it comes to stacking the tiles. However, most players would agree that the benefits of playing with a sumptuous set steeped in history outweigh the inconveniences. To play with the same set your parents or grandparents used, or with an antique set whose provenance is entirely unknown to you, makes for a magical journey of the senses wherein the distinct smell, sound, and feel of the tiles transport you to a different time or place. And that's worth a few tumbling tiles.

HAND-CARVED IVORY TILES, CIRCA 1923

IT'S ALL *in the* TOUCH

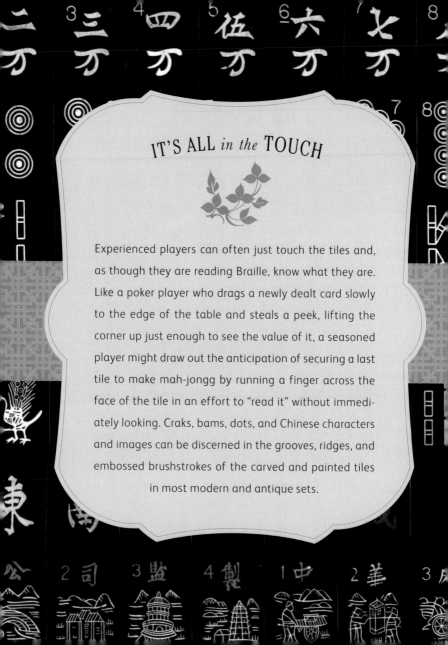

Experienced players can often just touch the tiles and, as though they are reading Braille, know what they are. Like a poker player who drags a newly dealt card slowly to the edge of the table and steals a peek, lifting the corner up just enough to see the value of it, a seasoned player might draw out the anticipation of securing a last tile to make mah-jongg by running a finger across the face of the tile in an effort to "read it" without immediately looking. Craks, bams, dots, and Chinese characters and images can be discerned in the grooves, ridges, and embossed brushstrokes of the carved and painted tiles in most modern and antique sets.

Some have tried to compare the mah-jongg tile to the domino, but this is like comparing Cinderella to her stepsisters. It's true that a tile is a tile and, like dominoes, mah-jongg pieces are small, chunky rectangular blocks, but that's where the similarities stop. The exquisite carving, etching, painting, and engraving of mah-jongg tiles can render the sets compact and practical works of art, emblazoned with dragons and birds of bright plumage among spring blossoms, colorful circles, and the painterly brushstrokes of calligraphy. Most of the sets being manufactured today are made of modern plastics meant to resemble ivory in look and feel, but in both the recent and distant past tiles were made of ivory, bone, bamboo, ebony, wood, celluloid, Bakelite, catalin, and even jade—all now, to various degrees, highly collectible materials.

The size of the tiles can range anywhere from about $^1/_8$ inch thick by $^1/_2$ inch wide by $^3/_4$ inch tall to 1 inch thick by $1^1/_4$ inches wide by $1^3/_4$ inches tall. Generally, Chinese and Vietnamese groups tend to enjoy playing with bigger, chunkier tiles; Americans and Europeans gravitate toward tiles that are medium sized; and Japanese players seem to prefer smaller, thicker tiles. As with the enjoyment of wine or food, in the end your choice basically comes down to what you like—and what's been put in front of you.

Both vintage and modern sets can be quite varied in hue, like wedding dresses, ranging in color from a rich butter to a brilliant snow, and beyond to include every color imaginable, from muted shades to garish hues. A visit to the replacement tile room at the National Mah Jongg League's headquarters in New York inspires flights of imagination as you stand surrounded by simple, beautiful rectangles of green jade, smoky bamboo, persimmon, pomegranate, ochre, sky, midnight, bone, and ivory. It's also interesting to note that players in Hong Kong seem to share with those in Miami a preference for wildly sassy tiles in bold Lee-Press-On-Nail colors.

The crafty rabbit has three different entrances to its lair.

~ Ancient Chinese proverb

VINTAGE SETS

Here is the stuff dreams are made of: Bakelite, catalin, celluloid, bone, ivory, vinyl plastics, jade, bamboo, and wood. If you're lucky enough to come across a Chinese set from circa 1920, it will likely be made of cow bone with bamboo backs and have been shipped from Shanghai to the West years ago during the mah-jongg boom.

Opening a vintage set and discovering the tiles' sumptuous material can be as exciting as opening presents on your birthday. Bakelite was the most common material used in American-made mah-jongg tiles during the 1920s and 1930s. Developed and patented in 1907 by Leo Baekeland, it was the first bona fide synthetic plastic. Shades range from a buttered-popcorn yellow to a creamy burnt orange, although other colors such as black and red were sometimes used and are evident in two-toned tiles. Bakelite tiles are quite opaque and dense, with rather sharp edges. The colorful designs were either carved by hand into the face or affixed by way of a molding process. Catalin is a refined version of Bakelite that was produced in the 1930s. Catalin tiles look very similar to those made of

TILE MATERIALS

IVORY	Visible dark and light lines create a wavy pearlescent grain on the front of the tile and a cross-hatched effect from the side.
JADE	Rare and not always of a brilliant green color.
BONE	Shows evidence of a network of small interconnecting channels in bone tissue.
CATALIN	Light buttered-popcorn yellow. Has rounder edges and appears more translucent and slightly lighter in color than Bakelite.
BAKELITE	Color ranges from buttered-popcorn yellow to a creamy burnt orange. Quite opaque and dense, with rather sharp edges.
CELLULOID	Man-made plastic and highly flammable (made from cellulose, a by-product of cotton).
BAMBOO	Features rougher carvings. Bamboo is often used as the backing of a plastic or bone tile.
WOOD	May be made of solid wood, painted or covered with paper, stickers, or plastic.

BAKELITE UP *up your* LIFE

One of the reasons for mah-jongg's leap in popularity among the hip and design savvy is due in large part to the use of Bakelite—a material sought by collectors—in vintage tiles. The recent surge in Bakelite's desirability has boosted the collectibility of vintage mah-jongg sets made of the beloved plastic. Created by Leo Baekeland in 1907 while he was developing a less-flammable bowling alley shellac, the heat- and pressure-formed material is quite tough and cannot be melted down again. Used first in automobile and industrial products, it later caught on with jewelry makers and industrial designers, blooming into an array of two hundred colors and looks, including translucent and marbelized. Bakelite applications range from homey flatware handles and kitchen items to fabulously sleek fashion accessories. During World War II, Bakelite manufacturers shifted their focus to support the war effort, incorporating the material into items such as aviator goggles. After the war, new technology produced cheaper, more advanced plastics, displacing the labor-intense substance from its position of popularity. Back in vogue for a while in the 1970s when artist Andy Warhol's affinity for the stuff inspired collectors and design lovers, it's now highly collectible again due to its enduring beauty.

Bakelite but have notably rounder edges and appear more translucent and slightly lighter in color.

Celluloid, developed in the 1860s, was one of the first man-made plastics and was highly flammable (made from cellulose, a by-product of cotton). It was developed as a cheap replacement for tortoiseshell and ivory and was used to make mah-jongg tiles, but when game sets began to be mass manufactured using cheaper, more advanced plastics, it fell by the way-side. For that reason, there aren't very many celluloid tiles still available.

Wood, boxwood, and composition wood were used to make the more affordable American sets as an alternative to the pricier imported versions made of bone and other materials considered precious. Some wooden tiles may be made of solid wood, flat on both sides and painted, carved, or covered with paper or stickers. Tiles in American-manufactured sets may also be composed of composition wood with paper or plastic tile fronts. And other tiles are made of boxwood with paper, celluloid, or other plastic faces. It may be surprising that solid bamboo, which makes gorgeous tiles, was actually used in less-expensive imported sets, but its abundance as a natural resource in China made it a logical choice

BONE *or* IVORY?

The best way to tell whether you're looking at bone or ivory is to conduct a visual test using a high-powered light and a jeweler's loupe. Close inspection of bone will turn up evidence of the *Haversian* system, named for English physician Clopton Havers (1655–1702). This is the network of small interconnecting channels in bone tissue through which blood vessels, nerve fibers, and lymphatics pass. These channels appear on a tile in the form of a straight grain and/or pores. Ivory, by comparison, will contain *Schreger lines*, named after Danish anatomist Heinrich Theodor Schreger (1768–1833). These are the dark and light lines visible under reflected light in a ground section of a tooth, as in those of mammoth or elephant tusks. These lines create a visible pattern that some describe as a wavy or pearlescent grain on the front of the tile, and a cross-hatched effect when viewed from the side. It is the presence or absence of this pattern that will tell you whether you are seeing ivory or bone.

HAND-CARVED JADE MAH-JONGG TILES
CIRCA 1920

of material. Bamboo has also been used as a back to other more precious materials, like bone, dating back to the early 1900s. It later inspired a trend from the 1960s to the 1980s wherein plastic tiles were often paired with bamboo backings, evoking the bone and bamboo tiles of yore. The carving on bamboo, for obvious reasons, is not as fine as on other materials. (*You* try carving a tiny bird with tiny feathers into a tiny chunk of rock-hard bamboo.)

Jade sets do exist, but they are rare and not always the brilliant green color you would expect; they come in mostly black and white varieties. The images on these tiles are all carved by hand. Bone, mainly derived from cattle, was the most common material used in the making of Chinese sets early in the twentieth century; nowadays a lot of sets coming from Shanghai are made of pulverized fish bone. Bone tiles of either sort are usually backed with bamboo, or sometimes ebony.

Ivory tiles can also be backed with bamboo or ebony, but solid ivory is immensely more valuable. If you're hoping to retire on the earnings from the sale of an antique ivory set and you've never heard of two guys named Havers and Schreger, you're going to need to get to know them (see "Bone or Ivory?" on page 83). You're also going to need a lot of luck, since ivory sets are *very* rare despite the number of sellers who claim to have one, two, or a dozen they wish to sell. One thing is for sure: you're going to have to kiss a lot of celluloid before you find an ivory prince. In fact, celluloid, sometimes called "French ivory," is quite often confused with the real thing due to its visible grain (known as Schreger lines), which is similar to that of true ivory.

HAND-CARVED BONE MAH-JONGG SET AND BOX, CIRCA 1920

LEE BURNETT'S NOODLE AND CHEESE KUGEL

Veteran mah-jongg player Lee Burnett has made a lot of kugel in her time. Here's her favorite recipe, confirmed to be delicious by her weekly mah-jongg circle.

Serves 6–8

- *4 eggs*
- *³/₄ cup sour cream*
- *1 teaspoon salt*
- *2 tablespoons sugar*
- *¹/₈ teaspoon nutmeg*
- *¹/₂ cup golden raisins*
- *2 cups cottage cheese*
- *5 cups cooked egg noodles*
- *2 tablespoons bread crumbs*
- *3 tablespoons melted butter*

Preheat the oven to 375°F. Butter a 2-quart baking dish or casserole.

Beat the eggs, sour cream, salt, and sugar together in a large mixing bowl. Stir in the nutmeg, raisins, cottage cheese, and noodles. Transfer to a baking dish or casserole. Sprinkle with the bread crumbs and drizzle with the melted butter.

Bake for 40 to 50 minutes, until the bread crumbs are browned.

TILE BASICS

Among the tiles there are three suits, sometimes referred to as the "common" tiles; each suit is made up of four sets, with each set numbered one through nine. One fundamental difference between American and Asian sets is the Arabic numerals located on one corner of the suit tiles (which, for non-Chinese speakers, means not having to play with the character translations scrawled on the palm of their hand). The following descriptions of the suit tiles refer to these numbers:

The circle tiles, or *dots*, as they are also called, are decorated with circles or dotlike shapes. The number of circles on a dot tile matches the numeral that appears on the corner of the tile.

The faces of the bamboo tiles, or *bams*, depict bamboo stalks. The number 1 tile, however, is often represented by a picture of a bird, usually a sparrow or lucky crane. As with the dot tiles, there is a number at the top of each tile, with the exception of the 8 bam, whose numeral usually appears in the center of the stalks of bamboo. The markings are generally green with an occasional dash of red on the 5, 7, and 9 tiles, but this color variation has no bearing on the game.

The character tiles, also known as *craks*, are each adorned with a Chinese symbol, always in red, each of which represents a Chinese numeral 1 through 9. (Players who do not read Chinese may find it especially useful to play with Arabic-numbered tiles of this suit.)

GOLDEN PORK POT STICKERS

Try this easy recipe for pot stickers, a kind of Chinese dumpling often served as dim sum. You can freeze any uncooked pot stickers for your next mah-jongg gathering.

Makes 48 dumplings

- $^1/_2$ head of cabbage

- 1 pound lean ground pork (ground beef or chicken may be substituted)

- $^1/_4$ cup finely chopped green onions

- 3 teaspoons salt

- 3 teaspoons finely ground, fresh peeled ginger

- 1 teaspoon sesame oil

- Dash of white pepper

- 48 pot sticker wrappers (or gyoza wrappers; most packages contain 50)

- $1^1/_2$ tablespoons vegetable oil

- $^1/_2$ cup water

Dipping Sauce

- $^1/_4$ cup soy sauce

- 1 teaspoon sesame oil

- 1 teaspoon white vinegar

- Dash of sugar

Cut the cabbage crosswise into thin strips. In a large bowl, mix the cabbage, ground pork, green onions, salt, ginger, sesame oil, and white pepper.

Place 1 tablespoon of the pork and cabbage mixture in the center of a pot sticker wrapper. Lightly wet the edges of the circular wrapper and fold it in half. Pinch the edges into pleats to create a pouch encasing the mixture. Repeat with the remaining wrappers and filling.

Heat 1 tablespoon of the vegetable oil in a large nonstick skillet. Place as many pot stickers as will fit in a single layer in the skillet (repeat all the following as necessary if cooking in batches) and pour $1/2$ cup of water over the top. Cover and cook them over medium-high heat for 7 minutes, or until the water is absorbed. (When reheating frozen pot stickers, repeat this water absorption step to fully reconstitute.)

Add another $1/2$ tablespoon vegetable oil to the skillet, and fry the pot stickers for 2 minutes (on one side only) or until the bottoms are golden brown.

To make the dipping sauce, in a small bowl, combine the soy sauce, sesame oil, white vinegar, and sugar. Serve with the pot stickers.

The *honor* tiles are divided into two groups, the *dragons* and the *winds*. There are three dragons: red, green, and white (also referred to as "soap"), with four identical tiles in each. The red dragon tiles are always red in color but can be graced with either the image of a dragon or the Chinese symbol *chung*, which means "center." And although the Chinese name for China is "Central Nation" (which might explain the meaning of the red dragon tiles), it is generally believed that the various symbols and characters have a stronger connection to the principles of ancient Chinese philosophy, astrology, and numerology, and may have had an influence in the formation of the occidental tarot.

The green dragons are also decorated with either the Chinese symbol *fa*, which loosely translates as "prosperity," or the image of a dragon. Both are always green in color. The white dragons, called *po* or "white" in Chinese, are completely blank (sometimes with a blue border), or they show a dragon outlined in blue or a geometric pattern.

Of the wind tiles there are four each of the following types: north, east, west, and south ("NEWS," as they are referred to on the annual National Mah Jongg League *Official Standard Hands and Rules* card). Each of these is marked with the Chinese character for one of the wind directions. As with the other tiles marked with Chinese symbols, engraved in the upper left-hand corner is the abbreviation for the wind direction, N, E, W, or S.

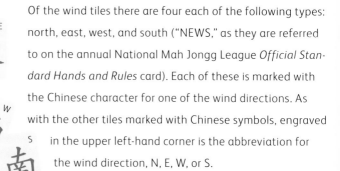

the lost art of

HAND-CARVED TILES

The beauty of vintage mah-jongg sets is the uniqueness of each hand-carved tile. Many Chinese artisans acquired their skills from their family's ancestral traditions of making mah-jongg sets. However, with dwindling demand for their skills and increasing demand for cheaper sets, these artisans cannot continue to practice a craft that dates back to the Qing dynasty. Furthermore, most of the tools needed are no longer being produced, and existing ones are fifty, sixty, or even seventy years old.

"The world is in danger of losing this craft," says Kristian Jansen Jaech, founder of Windfall Republic, a business dedicated to upholding the beauty of the truly handmade, hand-carved tile and saving this dying art. Today, Windfall Republic's small roster of artists (with two specializing in mah-jongg tile carving) are renowned for carving exquisite bird-themed, traditional, and bamboo sets in addition to customizing and carving single tiles, suits, replacement tiles, and entire sets incorporating whatever imagery is desired. (See the Resources section of this book for Windfall Republic's contact information.)

Adding to the overall beauty of the game are four *flower* and four *season* tiles (sometimes collectively referred to as *flower* tiles), which are considered optional for beginners in most Asian forms of play since they are not part of actual play but rather add bonus points onto total scores. These are generally used by experienced players for completing hands based on scoring systems that are more complicated than those used by beginners. These tiles come with the most variation from set to set. Some sets depict flowers, some mandarins, and some seasons—though they are generally all called "flower" tiles.

The eight "flower" tiles decorated with their different depictions of foliage are traditionally recognized as representing spring, summer, autumn, winter, plum, orchid, chrysanthemum, and bamboo (not related to the bams in the common tile grouping). Some mah-jongg sets include letter identifications in the upper left-hand corner of the flower or season tiles, but these labels are not essential to the game. If you play the American version of mah-jongg you will need to have all eight tiles in your set. Refer to the Resources section in this book if you find your set is lacking these tiles.

Lastly, you will not need *joker* tiles in the Asian versions of mah-jongg (except for the Shanghai version), but they are a part of the game in the American styles of play and thus are included in American sets. As is the case with the joker in a deck of cards, usually the word *joker* is emblazoned (in English) somewhere on the tile; often the word is accompanied by a Chinese character that translates to "one hundred uses." Eight jokers are required in order to play American mah-jongg. Though modern sets will come with the necessary number of jokers, this is not always the case with older sets. Joker decals, which can be attached to extra flower tiles or blanks, or actual joker tiles matching your set can be obtained through the National Mah Jongg League. Most modern Chinese sets come with four extras—blank white tiles similar to the white dragons— to be used in case a tile is lost; they can even be engraved with the design of the lost tile should that become necessary. Most modern American sets come with extra flower tiles for the same reasons. These tiles can be covered with decals (also available through the National Mah Jongg League) to replace a tile that is missing. (See the Resources section for the National Mah Jongg League's contact information as well as for information about custom tile engraving for replacements.)

MAH-JONGG *as* CRYSTAL BALL

The Chinese have long used various methods to divine their futures. Historians believe that one such method may have involved the use of dice and small pieces of wood—inscribed with the mystical symbols still found on modern mah-jongg tiles—which astrologers used to predict the movements of the celestial bodies by moving them around a board representing the heavens. Mah-jongg tiles as we know them today can also be used to read fortunes. Each dragon tile is thought to represent the powerful forces of the universe, with white indicating heaven, green symbolizing Earth (with its symbol for "prosperity"), and red representing man (with its symbol for "center"). Of the suit tiles, the dots represent the wheel of heaven, the bams the axis on which the Earth rotates, and the craks the infinite fates of man. The four winds are associated with four out of the five elements of the universe: east (wood), south (fire), west (metal), and north (water). Earth, the fifth element, is represented by the game's playing surface. The thirteen tiles of a player's hand relate to the lunar months in a year.

When divining with mah-jongg tiles, as with tarot, a reading involves a seeker, one who is looking for answers to personal questions, and a reader, one who knows how to interpret the cards, or tiles. The seeker shuffles the tiles and selects a number of them to be read (how many depends on the method of divination) and the reader lays out these chosen tiles in a pattern known as a spread. Each of the tiles has a name and general meaning attached; accuracy in reading depends on the diviner's skill, perceptivity, and faith. If a certain tile is repeated during a reading, its significance is believed to increase. And, as in tarot reading, certain symbols represent setbacks or problems. When tiles with these symbols crop up, another tile is drawn immediately afterward as a way of solving the problem using the symbol represented on that tile.

A mah-jongg tile and its associated meanings might be read and interpreted as follows:

5-dot

Name: DRAGON

Message: LASTING VALUES,

LONG-BINDING FRIENDSHIP,

JUSTICE, REWARDING WORK

2-crak

Name: SWORD

Message: DECISION,

QUANDARY, SEVERANCE,

TWINS, SEPARATION

There are also ways of reading tiles and futures through Chinese numerology. See the Resources section for recommended books on the topic of fortune-telling by way of mah-jongg.

TEA

When it comes to drinks at the mah-jongg table, we recommend going with a traditional Chinese tea. We prefer tea to coffee because coffee gives you a jolt of energy that tapers off quickly. Tea is also a great connector to Chinese history and a perfect refreshment for a game of mah-jongg.

TIPS FOR MAXIMIZING — YOUR BREW —

Use cold, filtered water

Bring water to a rolling boil (see recommended temperature for each type of tea)

Use loose-leaf teas whenever possible for the best flavor.

Use boiling water to rinse the teapot first, which will heat up the pot and prepare it for brewing.

Allow enough room for the tea leaves to expand and release their flavors.

WHITE

STEEP TIME: *4–15 minutes*
WATER TEMPERATURE: *185°F*
Not as common as Green Tea, White Tea has a hint of color, a subtle taste, and a wonderful rich smell. Perfect for those who want to enjoy tea with minimal caffeine.

GREEN

STEEP TIME: *2–3 minutes*
WATER TEMPERATURE: *160°F (when water bubbles begin to rise to the surface of the pot)*
Green Tea has a delicate, sweet, and fresh flavor.

OOLONG

STEEP TIME: *1–9 minutes*
WATER TEMPERATURE: *203°F (bring water to a full boil)*
Copper color. Deep, rich aroma.

BLACK

STEEP TIME: *3–5 minutes*
WATER TEMPERATURE: *203°F (bring water to a full boil)*
Dark amber color. Often Black Tea has a smoky and spicy flavor. Rich, full bodied.

TISANES & HERBAL

STEEP TIME: *5+ minutes*
WATER TEMPERATURE: *203°F (bring water to a full boil)*
Tisanes are teas infused with fruits, dried herbs, and natural flavors. Great to serve at a daytime mah-jongg game.

CHAPTER 3 ⊙ THE TRADITIONAL CHINESE AND AMERICAN GAMES

If you must play, decide on three things at the start: the rules of the game, the stakes, and the quitting time.

~ Traditional Chinese proverb

THE GAMES PEOPLE PLAY

DEDICATED PLAYERS OF TRADITIONAL CHINESE MAH-JONGG HAVE A DEEP REVERENCE FOR THE GAME, SEEING IT AS A GREAT METAPHOR FOR LIFE. THEY CLAIM THAT CERTAIN STRATEGIC MANEUVERS RESEMBLE REAL-LIFE CHALLENGES, WHEREIN FLEXIBILITY IS A VIRTUE, BECAUSE THINGS DON'T ALWAYS GO AS YOU WOULD LIKE. AND, AS IN LIFE, MUCH SKILL AND STRATEGY IS INVOLVED, BUT ALSO A LOT OF LUCK. IN CHINESE MAH-JONGG, THE RULES CAN DIFFER SO GREATLY FROM ONE VERSION TO ANOTHER, DEPENDING ON PLAYING STYLE AND INDIVIDUAL TASTES, THAT THE PLAYERS MUST COME TO A CONSENSUS BEFORE BEGINNING A GAME. ON THE OTHER HAND, MAH-JONGG AS IT IS PLAYED IN THE JEWISH AMERICAN COMMUNITY IS QUITE DIFFERENT IN CHARACTER.

As one Jewish player humorously confirmed, "The Jews took the game and codified it, made it rule bound, and *that's* what made it Jewish." Sometimes the two distinct styles of play make for amusing cultural interactions. In the film based on Amy Tan's novel *The Joy Luck Club*, the main character, Jing-mei, sits at her parents' kitchen table, occupying the seat of her recently deceased mother in a game of mah-jongg with her four "aunties"—her mother's longtime friends and mah-jongg partners. Auntie An-mei comments on Jing-mei's good fortune as she plays, saying that she wins just like her mother, to which Jing-mei replies, "I only played once with some Jewish friends in college." Hearing this, Auntie Lindo pipes in, "Ahhh, *Jewish* mah-jongg. Not the same thing. Entirely different."

SHE'S GOT GAME

Your mah-jongg set will in part determine whether you play the Chinese or American version of the game (you can play the traditional Chinese game and its Asian variants with an American set, but not vice versa). Or you may have a preference for one particular style based on experience, observation, tradition, or any number of other factors that will dictate which set you choose. If you're looking to join an existing group however, you'll need to learn the game that they are playing and any variations that they may have adopted. Beyond the traditional American and Chinese games, there are at least a dozen distinct styles to choose from, with countless offshoots and forms of the game that vary by style of play, culture, country, and even neighborhood and household. Main branches of play include traditional Chinese (Old Rules), Shanghai (New Rules), Taiwanese (Sixteen-Tile Game), Chinese Twelve-Tile, American

the
KIDS' TABLE

Although mah–jongg is considered by many Chinese families to be an essential part of the social fabric of everyday life, age and experience commonly define who plays at which table. Often, this means that at family gatherings there will be a table for adults, and a separate one for the "kids" (the term being loosely defined, however—"kids" may be as old as thirty-five). And because Chinese culture grants such honor to elders, younger players will often politely decline to play the highly competitive game of mah-jongg with their elders even when given the opportunity. There is a strong belief that one's true character is displayed at the mah-jongg table, and so it's not unusual, when one "meets the parents," to be asked to play mah-jongg with them (but after that, one is generally relegated to the kids' table).

(National Mah Jongg League rules), Wright-Patterson, Filipino, Japanese Classical, Japanese Modern, Korean, Malaysian, Nepalese, Singaporean, Vietnamese Classical, and Vietnamese Modern. The traditional Chinese game is considered the most straightforward and easiest to learn, and so it makes a good starting place for beginners. All versions of the Chinese game derive from the traditional Chinese style. Nearly all styles and variations are played with four players.

No matter which game you play, the objective is to be the first player to create a winning mah-jongg hand and declare, "mah-jongg!" To that end, the four players need to first determine their seating arrangements, build four walls of tiles, distribute thirteen tiles from the walls to each player (except the dealer, who gets fourteen), and draw and discard tiles to build a winning hand. If all the tiles from the walls are drawn and no one calls mah-jongg (called a "wall game"), the tiles are turned over and shuffled, and the process begins again with the next player (seated to the right) as dealer.

While the scoring of the Chinese version is more difficult to grasp than that of the American version, the game itself is easier to learn for beginners. The opposite is true in the American version, which changes every year with the issuance of the *Official Standard Hands and Rules* card by the National Mah Jongg League. To keep things interesting, the league recalibrates the hands for the coming year and lists new combinations and point values for scoring.

The basic setup procedures for the Chinese and American versions of play, described below, are quite similar. You can apply them to both games unless otherwise indicated. Consider learning the Chinese game first and then other games and styles—as in music, once you learn to read the notes, you can play many different songs.

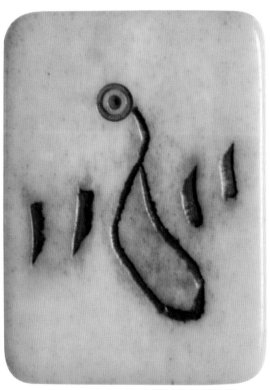

HAND-CARVED ONE-BAM TILE IN BONE, QIN DYNASTY

HOW TO PLAY TRADITIONAL CHINESE MAH-JONGG—
SIMPLIFIED RULES

Yes! You can learn to play mah-jongg. The traditional Chinese game uses 144 tiles, divided into two categories:

HONOR TILES

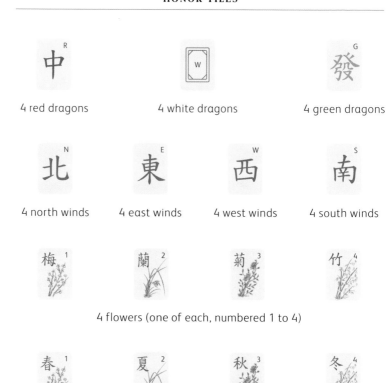

4 red dragons   4 white dragons   4 green dragons

4 north winds   4 east winds   4 west winds   4 south winds

4 flowers (one of each, numbered 1 to 4)

4 seasons (one of each, numbered 1 to 4)

36 craks (four of each number 1 through 9)

36 dots (four of each number 1 through 9)

36 bams (four of each number 1 through 9)

Regardless of how many extra tiles you have or whether you can identify all of the tiles in your particular set (for example, you may not be able to distinguish a blank tile from a white dragon), all that's required for play is a simple consensus among the players regarding the tiles' meaning.

Courtesy
DON'T TAP A PLAYER ON THE SHOULDER DURING A GAME. IT'S BAD LUCK.

The East is where things begin, my mother once told me,
the direction from which the sun rises, where the wind comes from.

~ *Amy Tan,* The Joy Luck Club

Game Setup
Step 1: Determining Seating and Choosing A Dealer

Some Chinese practitioners of feng shui—the philosophy of using spatial arrangement to maximize the beneficial flow of energy—believe that a person's luck is influenced by their position within their environment and the objects that surround them. For these players, seating positions in relation to doors, windows, and traffic patterns in the room can be extremely important. Consequently, Chinese players will often determine who sits where before determining who will serve as first dealer. An easy way to do both at once is to take a tile representing each wind (north, east, west, and south), place them face down, shuffle them, and ask each player to select one. The player who selects the east wind (the luckiest wind) can choose his or her seating position as well as serve as the initial east wind (and dealer) of the game; the other players sit at the table in relation to the east wind according to the winds designated on their tiles (north sits to east's right, west sits opposite, and south sits to east's left) and will play these respective winds at the outset of the game. This method has the added benefit of randomizing who sits next to whom, so that players inclined to pass beneficial discard tiles to one another may not necessarily be sitting in the optimal positions. If feng shui is not an essential part of your play, and you have no reason to suspect collusion among players, let everyone sit where they like and consider letting the host or hostess serve as the initial east wind.

East serves as the dealer of the *hand* (defined as the duration of a single deal of the tiles). If the initial east wind player *mah-jonggs* (wins the hand), she deals the next hand. Otherwise, the east wind (the job of dealer) rotates counterclockwise to the next player for the next hand. In other words, without anyone moving seats, the deal is passed from one player to the next in a counterclockwise fashion. A *round* is completed once the dealer duties have rotated around the table to all four players and return to the initial east player. At the outset of a session, players will generally agree to play a set number of rounds that will constitute a complete *game*.

To the potential confusion of beginners, there is also an overall prevailing wind—different from the players' wind assignments for that hand—which presides over each *round* of play. At the beginning of a game, a prevailing wind indicator is placed at the seating position of the player who is the first dealer (the initial east position). This wind indicator remains at the seat of the first dealer for the duration of the game. Before the first hand is played, an adjustable element in the wind indicator (usually a tiny die or dial) is set to east. At the end of each round of play (when the deal returns to the initial dealer), the element in the wind indicator is adjusted to indicate south, which becomes the prevailing wind of that round. In subsequent rounds, the wind is set to west, then north, then (if the game is to continue) back to east, and so on. Some sets also come with a first dealer indicator, but most players let the prevailing wind indicator, staying in place by the initial dealer, serve dual purpose. The winds, both the players' and the prevailing, have significance in the scoring of the Chinese game but no particular significance in the American game (other than the extra tile given to the east player/dealer at the outset of the hand).

Step 2: Shuffling the Tiles and Building the Wall

Once you have determined seating arrangements and wind assignments, it's time to shuffle the tiles. Turn all the tiles face down (including the four wind tiles used to determine seating) and shuffle, or "wash," them by vigorously and thoroughly mixing them so that no player can tell which tile is which. Each player then takes thirty-six tiles (keeping them face down) and builds a stack of tiles eighteen long by two high. These four long stacks are then pushed to the center of the table to form a square known as the *wall*. (The process of building the wall is the same in the American version of play, but the additional eight joker tiles included in American sets mean that the players must each take thirty-eight tiles for a stack nineteen tiles long. The racks used in American mah-jongg can come in handy for pushing the tiles forward and building the wall neatly.)

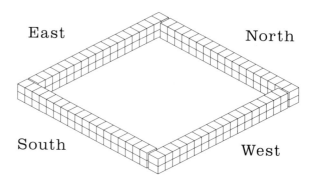

Off-the-wall
PARTY TRICK

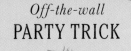

In the Chinese game, where racks (often used to push tiles forward neatly to form the wall) are not customarily used, impress the players around you (or humiliate yourself publicly) by attempting to pick up an entire row of eighteen tiles using only your hands. Simply create a row of eighteen tiles and another one in front of it. (Lift the farther row and place it on top of the nearer row.) By stretching your fingers wide over as many tiles as possible and applying pressure to the two ends with your pinkies, you will be able to lift and move an entire row. Squeeze, lift, and hope for the best. This is a very impressive trick, if you can pull it off.

Step 3: Breaking the Wall

Next comes the process of drawing the tiles from the wall. To determine which tiles are taken and drawn by players, the east wind (the dealer) throws three dice within the confines of the wall and adds up the dice's total to determine where to open the wall. Keeping in mind this total, the dealer counts the sides of the wall counterclockwise starting with his or her own side and continues around until the total roll of the dice is reached.

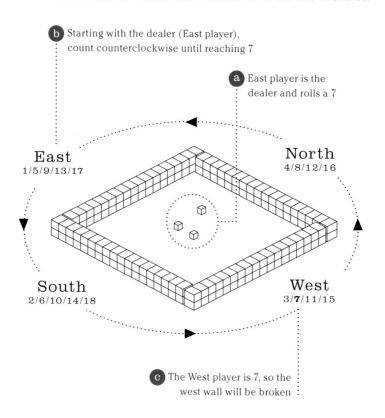

b Starting with the dealer (East player), count counterclockwise until reaching 7

a East player is the dealer and rolls a 7

East
1/5/9/13/17

North
4/8/12/16

South
2/6/10/14/18

West
3/**7**/11/15

c The West player is 7, so the west wall will be broken

The dealer then uses the same number to determine where that side of the wall will be broken. In the example below, the dealer would count seven stacks in from the right of the west wall and then take two stacks (four tiles) to the left of that spot. Each player then proceeds in a counterclockwise direction taking the next group of two stacks (four tiles) to the left of the break until each player has twelve tiles. (Although play order and the order in which players draw tiles is counterclockwise, tiles are removed from the wall in a clockwise direction from the left of the break.) The dealer then draws two more tiles by taking one tile, skipping the next three tiles, and taking the following one to form a total hand

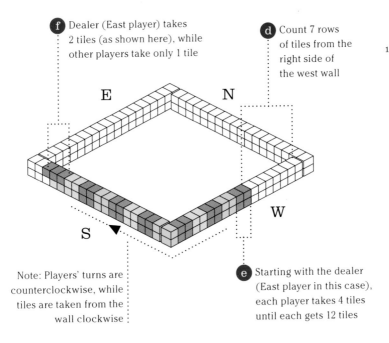

f Dealer (East player) takes 2 tiles (as shown here), while other players take only 1 tile

d Count 7 rows of tiles from the right side of the west wall

Note: Players' turns are counterclockwise, while tiles are taken from the wall clockwise

e Starting with the dealer (East player in this case), each player takes 4 tiles until each gets 12 tiles

of fourteen tiles (see diagram). The south, west, and north players each draw one additional tile in the following order: bottom, top of next stack, bottom of next stack. They will now have thirteen tiles each, while the dealer enjoys the advantage of holding fourteen tiles. After the tiles have all been distributed, players turn their tiles toward them, placing them on end in a neat line. Setup is now finished and it's time to play.

> *Courtesy*
> CAST THE DICE INSIDE THE CONFINES OF THE WALLS
> ONCE THEY ARE BUILT.

Step 4: Removing the Flower and Season Tiles

In the Chinese form of play, flower and season tiles are not instrumental in *playing*, but rather in scoring. They are not included as part of a winning hand, but rather are incorporated in the form of points added or deducted once a player declares mah-jongg. (For this reason, some beginning players will remove the tiles before the "wash" and not include them in play. The instructions that follow include them in the game.)

Once setup is finished, all players must review their hands and expose any flower or season tiles they may have, placing them face up to their left on the table. They then draw a makeup tile from the end of the "dead wall" (the portion of the wall to the right of where the tiles were removed at the beginning of a hand; see diagram). Players without flower or season tiles simply skip this step.

If a player's makeup tile happens to be another flower or season tile, that player must wait until all other players make up for their flower or season tiles before she can draw a second makeup tile from the end of the dead wall.

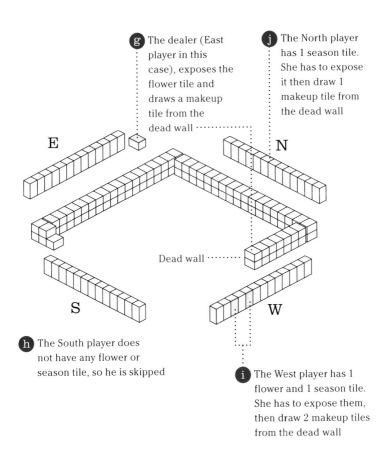

g The dealer (East player in this case), exposes the flower tile and draws a makeup tile from the dead wall

j The North player has 1 season tile. She has to expose it then draw 1 makeup tile from the dead wall

E

N

Dead wall

S

W

h The South player does not have any flower or season tile, so he is skipped

i The West player has 1 flower and 1 season tile. She has to expose them, then draw 2 makeup tiles from the dead wall

Players may sometimes draw a flower or season tile during a game. If this happens, the player must immediately expose the flower or season tile by placing it face up to his or her left and then draw a makeup tile from the dead wall. If the makeup tile turns out to be *another* flower or season, the player must immediately expose it and draw a second makeup tile from the dead wall. Because the flower is obtained by having drawn a tile from the wall during normal play, the player who drew it must discard an unwanted tile and then it's the next player's turn.

Note: There are only two situations in which a player draws a tile from the dead wall: after exposing a kong (as described on page 123) and when drawing a makeup tile after exposing a flower or season tile, as described above.

FLOWER POWER

A player can use flower or season tiles (or the lack of them) to earn additional points at the end of a hand in several ways: by having no flower or season tiles, by having flower or season tiles that match his or her seating position (for example, flower tile 1 drawn by the east position, flower tile 2 drawn by the south position, and so on), or by having all four flowers or all four seasons. Any player who accumulates seven or eight flower or season tiles in one game is considered to have completed his or her hand and therefore wins the game. (7 flowers will yield a 3 fan game while 8 flowers will yield a 4 fan game. See section on scoring later in this chapter.)

Rules of Play

The dealer starts the game by removing one of his or her tiles that doesn't seem useful or doesn't match the others. The dealer takes this tile and places it face up in the center of the table, where it is surrounded by the four walls. The dealer, like the other players, now has thirteen tiles. The dealer's turn is over, and the next turn belongs to the south wind player, to the right of the dealer. The south wind player draws a tile from the wall and can either discard the tile by placing it face up in the center of the wall or keep it. If that player wants to keep the tile, he or she needs to discard an unwanted tile from the other thirteen tiles in his or her hand. Once that player discards a tile, it becomes the next player's turn. The game moves counterclockwise from one player to another; tiles are drawn from the wall in a clockwise fashion and unwanted tiles are discarded as each player attempts to create a winning mah-jongg hand. Discarded tiles are up for grabs by other players, as described later in this chapter.

As in the game gin rummy, where the object is to arrange cards in sequential and matching sets for a win, you must obtain a complete mah-jongg hand before the other players do in order to prevail. A winning mah-jongg hand is composed of four groupings (of three or four tiles each) and a pair (called "eyes"). These groupings are called chows, pungs, and kongs.

What's in a Chow?

A *chow* is a group of three tiles of the same suit in a sequence, or run.

   Example: 1-bam, 2-bam, and 3-bam constitute a chow.

GINGER MILK CUSTARD

This easy-to-make Chinese dessert
is a perfect late-night snack.

Serves 4

- *4 ounces fresh ginger*
  (to yield 4 tablespoons ginger juice)

- *4 cups whole milk, chilled*

- *Sugar (approximately 1 tablespoon)*

Finely grate the ginger. Push the ginger pulp through a strainer and reserve the juice. Pour 1 tablespoon of the ginger juice into each of four small rice bowls. Set aside.

Heat the milk until tepid. Slowly pour the sugar into the milk to your liking. Stir gently until the sugar is completely dissolved.

Swiftly pour 1 cup of the milk into each of the bowls. Do not stir. Let sit for 3 minutes.

Serve the custard warm.

There are two different kinds of chows, which are obtained in different ways, described below.

Concealed Chow

The *concealed chow* is achieved by drawing a tile from the wall during your turn, forming a group of three sequential tiles.

> *Example:* It's your turn to draw from the wall. You currently have a 2-bam and a 3-bam in your hand and draw a 1-bam from the wall to create a 1-2-3-bam concealed chow. From your hand you then choose a tile that you don't need and discard it in the middle of the wall, face up.

A concealed chow is held in a player's hand, without being revealed to the other players. If the player declares mah-jongg, the hand is then revealed to the other players.

Exposed Chow

The *exposed chow* is achieved by claiming a tile discarded by the player whose turn was immediately before yours.

> *Example:* The player seated to your left discards a 1-bam. You currently have a 2-bam and a 3-bam in your hand, so claiming the discarded 1-bam would give you an exposed chow. To claim the discarded 1-bam, say, "Chow," pick up the 1-bam, and expose your 2- and 3-bam tiles. Move the exposed 1-2-3-bam chow to your left side and discard an unwanted tile. It's now the next player's turn.

An exposed chow is revealed for all players to see. Once tiles are exposed, they remain exposed throughout the entire hand.

What's in a Pung?

A *pung* is a group of three identical tiles.

Example: Three red dragon tiles or three 6-dot tiles constitute a pung.

Once again, there are two different kinds of pungs, obtained in different ways.

Concealed Pung

The *concealed pung* is achieved by drawing a tile (to match two tiles in your hand) from the wall during your turn.

> *Example:* It's your turn to draw from the wall. You currently have two 1-dot tiles in your hand and draw another 1-dot from the wall to create a 1-dot concealed pung. From your hand you then choose a tile that you don't need and discard it in the middle of the wall, face up. It's now the next player's turn.

Exposed Pung

The *exposed pung* is achieved by claiming a tile (to match two tiles in your hand) discarded by any one of the players. Because a player can "pung" a tile discarded by any player, this means that one or several players' turns may be skipped.

> *Example:* The player across from you discards a 1-dot. You currently have two 1-dot tiles in your hand, so the discarded 1-dot added to your pair would create a 1-dot exposed pung. To claim the discarded 1-dot, say, "Pung!" pick up the 1-dot, and expose your own 1-dot tiles. Move the 1-dot exposed pung to your left side and discard an unwanted tile. It's now the next player's turn (the player to your right).

What's in a Kong?

A *kong* is composed of four identical tiles.

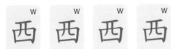

Example: Four west wind tiles constitute a kong.

Kongs are governed by two special rules: 1) A kong must be exposed before mah-jongg is declared (a hand is won); and 2) once a kong has been exposed, the player must draw a tile from the dead wall. In effect, the player who exposes a kong gets to draw two tiles—one from the wall or discard pile, and then one from the dead wall after the exposure of a kong.

There are several ways of obtaining a kong.

Concealed Kong

A *concealed kong* is achieved by having three identical tiles in your hand and drawing a fourth identical tile from the wall when it is your turn. At that moment, you have two options: to expose the kong immediately or keep the kong concealed.

⊙ To expose the kong immediately, say, "Kong!" as you draw the fourth identical tile and expose all four tiles. After moving them to the left, draw one tile from the dead wall and discard an unwanted tile. It then becomes the next player's turn.

⊙ Alternatively, you may keep the kong concealed and expose it at a later time. As you draw a fourth identical tile, simply keep it concealed in your hand, and discard an unwanted tile. It is then the next player's turn. However, to mah-jongg, all concealed kongs must be exposed prior to declaring a win. To do so, wait until it is your turn, draw a tile from the wall, declare, "Kong!" and expose your kong. Move the four identical tiles to your left, draw a tile from the dead wall, and discard an unwanted tile. It's now the next player's turn.

The reasons for holding on to a concealed kong rather than exposing it are:

⊙ To let other players chase after a tile when you already possess all four, thus preventing them from ever getting a winning hand.

⊙ To save one of the identical tiles for a possible chow later.

> *Example:* You have four 1-crak tiles, a 2-crak, and a 3-crak. The best way to utilize the 1-crak tiles is not to expose a kong but rather to split them to form a concealed 1-crak pung and a concealed 1-2-3 crak chow.

Exposed Kong

An *exposed kong* is achieved by claiming a tile (to match three identical tiles in your hand) discarded by any one of the players.

> *Example:* The player to the right of you discards a 4-bam. You currently have three 4-bam tiles in your hand, so you can use the discarded 4-bam to create an exposed 4-bam kong. To claim the discarded 4-bam, say, "Kong!" and then pick up the 4-bam and expose your own 4-bam tiles. Move the exposed 4-bam pung to your left side on the table and discard an unwanted tile. It's now the next player's turn.

However, as is the case with a concealed kong, you have two options 1) Declare, "Kong," and proceed as described in the example above, 2) alternatively, don't expose the kong at this time; instead, expose a pung and save one of the identical tiles for a possible chow later on.

Example: A player discards a 4-bam. You currently have one 2-bam, one 3-bam, and three 4-bam tiles. The best way to utilize the four 4-bam tiles in this case is not to expose a kong, but rather to split them to form an exposed 4-bam pung and a concealed 2-3-4-bam chow. So you call out "Pung!" pick up the discarded 4-bam tile, and expose two of the three 4-bams you have in your hand, saving one to create a concealed 2-3-4 bam chow. Finally, you discard an unwanted tile. It's now the next player's turn.

Exposing a Kong Later

If at any point you decide you don't need the tile you've been saving to create a chow, you can discard it as an unwanted tile or, better yet, expose it and declare a kong, if possible. This allows you a chance to draw a tile from the dead wall.

Example: You have an exposed 4-bam pung on the table, and one 4-bam tile in your hand. It's now your turn to draw a tile, and you decide that you don't need the 4-bam after all. Draw a tile from the wall as usual, declare "Kong!" and expose the 4-bam tile by placing it next to your exposed 4-bam pung to create an exposed 4-bam kong. Then draw a tile from the dead wall and discard an unwanted tile. It's now the next player's turn.

WHY BOTHER *to* KONG?

Since kongs can be complex and difficult to understand, you may be wondering why players use them at all. The answer is that kongs can be used strategically to gain advantage during a game. Kongs can be used to do the following:

⊙ Deny other players the chance to claim a particular tile

⊙ Give you an extra chance to draw a new tile from the dead wall

⊙ Disrupt the flow of the game and the order of other players' turns when you draw a tile from the discard pile

PUNG CHOW
"The Set with the Real Dragons"

This $35.00 set (Style 500) is most popular.

Style 351   Price $20.00

A complete set of 144 black walnut tiles (standard size), with black pyralin backs and ivory pyralin faces.

In classic Chinese designs in three rich Oriental colors, brilliant and permanent. Packed in a beautiful wooden box of Chinese style, with trays and full equipment of pyralin counters, dice, score cards and instruction book.

Style 376   Price $25.00

A complete set of 144 boxwood tiles (standard size), with extra heavy pyralin faces.

In three Oriental colors of brilliant and indelible hue. This combination of box-wood back with pyralin face has a striking Chinese appearance, and is at the same time superior in workmanship and finish to the imported bone and bamboo tiles.

Packed in an appropriate box of Chinese style, with trays, full equipment of pyralin counters, dice, score cards and instruction book.

PUNG CHOW
—the most beautiful game in the world.

A splendid addition to any home is this set $75.00 (Style 700)

Style 500   Price $35.00

A complete set of 144 solid ivory pyralin tiles (standard size), with black backs. The classic designs in three Oriental colors are particularly beautiful and permanent.

All solid pyralin tiles are unbreakable and can be fully cleansed in water without the slightest impairment of the indelible coloring of the designs.

Packed in a handsome leather covered box of special design with rich metal handles and mountings, with tray for tiles and four individual counter trays. Full equipment of pyralin counters, dice, score cards and instruction book.

Style 700   Price $75.00

A complete set of 144 *de luxe* tiles of solid grained ivory pyralin, richly and deeply engraved in classic Chinese designs and painted in three Oriental colors.

These tiles are of especial thickness and weight. Packed in a beautiful mahogany box, hand-finished, of the finest workmanship, with four trays to hold the tiles and four individual counter trays. Full equipment of pyralin counters, dice, score cards and instruction book.

Eyes to Win

Eyes, a pair of identical tiles needed to complete a mah-jongg hand, can be obtained in two ways: by drawing a tile from the wall, or by claiming a discarded tile immediately before declaring a mah-jongg.

Example: You have the following tiles in your hand: a 1-2-3-bam chow, a 4-crak pung, three west winds pung, a 4-5-6-dot chow, and a white dragon. The only thing standing between you and victory is an additional white dragon to complete the pair of eyes.

Situation A: It's your turn and you draw a white dragon from the wall. You now have a winning hand and so you declare, "Mah-jongg!"

Situation B: It's your turn, and you draw a tile from the wall, but it's not a white dragon. You discard the unwanted tile. The next player draws a tile and discards a white dragon. You claim the discarded white dragon to complete your pair of eyes and declare, "Mah-jongg!"

Courtesy

THE BEST TIME TO LEAVE THE TABLE IS WHEN A ROUND HAS BEEN COMPLETED (I.E., ALL FOUR PLAYERS HAVE BEEN DEALER AND THE WIND INDICATOR IS PASSED TO THE NEXT PLAYER IN LINE). INTERRUPTING THE GAME IS BELIEVED TO BRING BAD LUCK TO THE WINNER AND GOOD LUCK TO THE PERSON WHO CAUSED THE INTERRUPTION.

> *Courtesy*
>
> DETERMINE YOUR NEXT DISCARD WHILE WAITING FOR YOUR TURN,
> SO YOU WON'T MAKE OTHERS WAIT.

Rules for Picking Up a Discarded Tile

If a player's discarded tile benefits your hand, take it, but keep in mind the following restrictions:

⊙ Only the most recently discarded tile can be claimed.

⊙ You must grab it quickly. It is only available until the next player makes a move.

⊙ You can only take someone's discarded tile if:

     a) it completes one of your three-tile or four-tile groupings

     b) makes for a mah-jongg

     c) completes a pair of eyes that makes a complete winning hand.

You cannot take a discard and add it to your hand for later use:

⊙ If the discarded tile completes a chow in your hand, you may only use it if the player before you has discarded it. If the discarded tile completes a pung or a kong, you may use it regardless of who discarded it.

⊙ It is poor etiquette—you may also appear to be cheating—if you take a discarded tile and place it in your hand before exposing the grouping it completes. When you take the discarded tile from its face-up position in the center of the table, you must place it face up to your left and lay the rest of the tiles in the grouping beside it so that it's visible to all players.

Using a Discard to Win Mah-Jongg

If you're on the verge of having a complete hand (winning mah-jongg) and taking a discard would mean victory, then by all means do it, regardless of whose turn it is. Immediately shout, "Mah-jongg!" Claim the discarded tile and expose all of your tiles for the other players to inspect.

When two or more players need the same tile, here is how you determine who is entitled to the tile:

⊙ Pungs and kongs take precedence over chows.

⊙ Mah-jonggs take precedence over all.

⊙ If two or more players require the same tile for a mah-jongg, the player whose turn comes next in the rotation after the discarder claims it.

A No-Win Situation

Sometimes nobody wins. This circumstance, known as a *wall game* or a *drawn round*, occurs when no tiles are left in the wall and play ceases. And that's when you reshuffle the tiles and start all over. The initial dealer retains the deal.

Score!

Many groups come up with their own ways of scoring, especially at first, because in Chinese mah-jongg this process can be somewhat complicated. In the beginning it's more important to just learn to play. You can study the intricacies of scoring as you advance. For starters, here are a couple of options, the first being perhaps the easiest:

⊙ Dole out some chips, small tokens, or actual small coins and then establish a rule that the winner receives a chip or coin from every player (the same amount regardless of the winning hand).

⊙ To make things more competitive, you can add qualifications, such as the following:

> *Example:* If the winning tile was self-drawn (from the wall), every player gives the winner two chips or coins. If the winning tile was discarded by a particular player, then that player pays the winner two chips or coins while the other players pay one.

As you get more acquainted and adventurous with the game, you can try the Chinese scoring system. In this system, additional points, or "fans," as they are called, are awarded for harder-to-acquire hands, for pungs or kongs using certain honor tiles, and for various quantities and types of flower and season tiles.

Courtesy
KEEP YOUR EMOTIONS IN CHECK. IT IS JUST AS IMPORTANT TO WIN
GRACIOUSLY AS IT IS TO LOSE GRACIOUSLY.

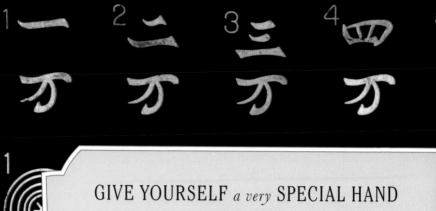

GIVE YOURSELF *a very* SPECIAL HAND

Most beginners tend to focus on fairly straightforward combinations of tiles—the easiest being the "chicken hand." A combination of chows and pungs of various suits and a pair, the chicken hand is the easiest hand to acquire (see following pages). In fact, the chicken hand is so easy that in the Chinese scoring system it isn't worth anything. Most veteran groups won't even allow chicken hands in the game. But during their first few mah-jongg sessions, beginning players will get very familiar and comfortable with the chicken.

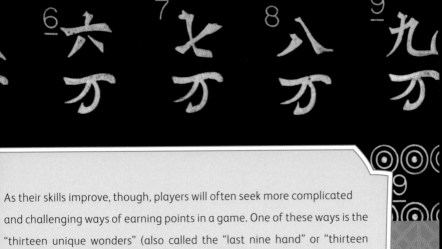

As their skills improve, though, players will often seek more complicated and challenging ways of earning points in a game. One of these ways is the "thirteen unique wonders" (also called the "last nine hand" or "thirteen orphans"), which is generally worth the maximum number of fans in any given game. For the Chinese, this practically impossible-to-acquire hand is so good that it's bad. It's believed that in order to achieve it one uses up every bit of one's good luck for the whole year—resulting in a win of the hand and perhaps the game, but also a perilous year. To be so lucky as to be cursed for the rest of the year, you need to get one of each of the 1 and 9 tiles of each suit, one of each of the winds, one of each of the dragons, and a fourteenth tile that matches one of the others in the hand. All the tiles must be picked up from the wall except the fourteenth tile, which may be taken from a discard.

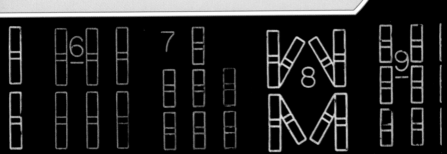

CHINESE MAH-JONGG HANDS *and* FAN VALUES

NAME	DESCRIPTION	FAN
CHICKEN HAND	Pungs, kongs, chows, and a pair of eyes in a variety of suits.	0
COMMON HAND	All chows and a pair of eyes in a variety of suits.	1
TRIPLET HAND	Pungs, kongs, and a pair of eyes in a variety of suits.	3
MIX ONE SUIT	Pungs, kongs, chows, and a pair of eyes of the same suit with honor tiles.	3
PURE ONE SUIT	Pungs, kongs, and chows of the same suit.	6
PURE ONE SUIT TRIPLETS	All pungs and kongs of the same suit.	9

As a beginner, you'll be playing the Chicken hand most of the time.
But as you get more accustomed to the game, challenge yourself and your
playing partners with the more difficult hands.

EXAMPLE

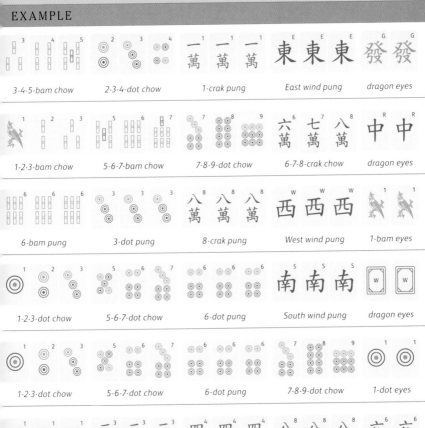

3-4-5-bam chow	2-3-4-dot chow	1-crak pung	East wind pung	dragon eyes
1-2-3-bam chow	5-6-7-bam chow	7-8-9-dot chow	6-7-8-crak chow	dragon eyes
6-bam pung	3-dot pung	8-crak pung	West wind pung	1-bam eyes
1-2-3-dot chow	5-6-7-dot chow	6-dot pung	South wind pung	dragon eyes
1-2-3-dot chow	5-6-7-dot chow	6-dot pung	7-8-9-dot chow	1-dot eyes
1-crak pung	3-crak pung	4-crak pung	9-crak pung	6-crak eyes

MAXIMIZE YOUR HAND

NAME	DESCRIPTION	FAN
THIRTEEN UNIQUE WONDERS	1- and 9-bam, -crak and -dot; one of each of the honor tiles; and one of the above to form the eyes.	maximum set by players
JUNIOR THREE CHIEFS	Pung or kong of two dragons and one pair of the other dragon to form the eyes.	1 fan less than the maximum set by players
GRAND THREE CHIEFS	Pung or kong of all three dragons.	maximum set by players
JUNIOR FOUR HAPPINESS	Pung or kong of three winds and one pair of the other wind to form the eyes.	1 fan less than the maximum set by players
GRAND FOUR HAPPINESS	Pungs, kongs, and chows of the same suit.	maximum set by players
EIGHTEEN MONKS	All kongs and one pair of eyes in a variety of suits (please note that winner will end up with 18 tiles instead of 14).	maximum set by players

Should you be so lucky as to encounter one of the following hands, you will be given the maximum amount of fan. At the beginning of the game, all players must agree on the maximum fan of a hand (usually 8 or 12 fan).

EXAMPLE

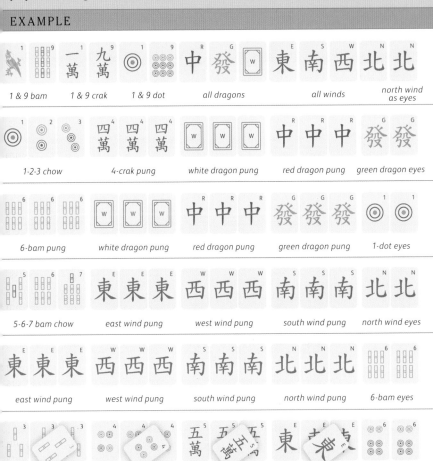

| 1 & 9 bam | 1 & 9 crak | 1 & 9 dot | all dragons | all winds | north wind as eyes |

| 1-2-3 chow | 4-crak pung | white dragon pung | red dragon pung | green dragon eyes |

| 6-bam pung | white dragon pung | red dragon pung | green dragon pung | 1-dot eyes |

| 5-6-7 bam chow | east wind pung | west wind pung | south wind pung | north wind eyes |

| east wind pung | west wind pung | south wind pung | north wind pung | 6-bam eyes |

| 3-bam kong | 4-dot kong | 5-crak kong | East wind kong | 6-dot eyes |

ADD AN EXTRA FAN TO YOUR HAND

NAME	DESCRIPTION	ADD'L F
NO FLOWER OR SEASON	Winner did not get any flower or season tiles during the hand.	+1
CORRESPONDING FLOWER OR SEASON	Winner gets a flower and/or season tile that corresponds to his seat position (counting 1 to 4, counterclockwise starting with the dealer as 1).	+1 for flow +1 for seas (max. +2)
SEAT POSITION WIND	Winner has a pung or kong of the wind of her seating position.	+1
PREVAILING WIND	Winner has a pung or kong of the prevailing wind (this is shown on the prevailing wind indicator).	+1
DRAGONS	Pung or kong of any one or two dragons (see previous page for hands with three dragons).	+1 per each dragon
SELF-DRAWN WINNER	Winner draws the tile to complete a mah-jongg.	+1

In addition to the fan allotted to a hand, players can get additional fans added to their hand as shown below.

EXAMPLE

Chicken Hand (0) + No flowers or seasons (+1) = 1 fan

Player seated across from dealer has a 3-flower (+1) + Pure One Suit (6 fans) = 7 fans

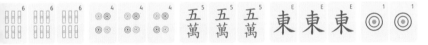

Dealer seated in East seat pungs east wind (+1) + All Triplet Hand (3) = 4 fans

Chicken Hand (0) + Pung of the prevailing wind, south (+1) = 1 fan

Chicken Hand (0) + Pung of the green dragon (+1) = 1 fan

Chicken Hand (0) + Pung of the red dragon (+1) + Self-drawn 4-crak (+1) = 2 fans

The FUNKY CHICKEN

Which came first, the chicken or the yakitori tile? Players of the modern Japanese game often incorporate "yakitori markers" as an additional fun way of scoring points on a hand. *Yakitori* (which means "roasted bird"), or roasted chicken on a stick, is a very popular street food in Japan and in Japantowns in other countries, especially during festivals, and it is served as the main event in restaurants specializing in this savory snack. Yakitori markers in mah-jongg depict a skewered chicken on one side. Each player gets a marker, which is left chicken-side up during play. When a player wins a hand, he or she "flips his chicken," turning the marker over. At the end of the game, if someone still has his or her skewered chicken facing up (meaning he or she has not won a single hand), that player must pay a special penalty to the other players with flipped chickens. (See the Resources section if you want to acquire these fun but optional pieces.)

If your group wants to play for money you'll need to establish a monetary base. Here's a suggestion:

> *Example:* Establish a base unit of ten cents per fan. A two-fan hand would then be worth twenty cents ($0.10 x 2), and a three-fan hand would be worth thirty cents ($0.10 x 3). By increasing the fan value of your hand, you increase your winnings.

Once the monetary base has been established, you'll need to figure out how many fans your hand is worth. As shown in the chart on pages 134–135, the "pure one suit" hand is worth six fans. The common hand is is worth one fan. Bonus points are also awarded to your basic hand for a variety of reasons (see the chart on pages 138–139).

> If you are the winner, tally up all your fans plus bonus points, multiply that total by $0.10, and prepare to be paid that amount by all players.

According to the traditional Chinese scoring rules, if you win mah-jongg from a self-drawn tile, everyone must pay you double the value of your hand. If a particular player discarded the tile you used to complete your winning hand, then that player pays you double while the other players pay the actual worth of your hand.

Study the basic hands, fans, and additional bonus points and watch your money grow—and your skills improve!

Courtesy
IT IS BEST TO PAY THE WINNER OF EACH HAND AS SOON AS THE HAND
IS WON. STRANGELY ENOUGH, UNPAID DEBT IS BELIEVED TO BRING
BAD LUCK TO THE WINNER (BUT NOT THE LOSER).

PUT YOUR MONEY *to* GOOD USE!

Although the scoring in American mah-jongg is generally a little less complicated than that in Chinese mah-jongg, many people choose to devise their own methods of scoring and paying out. One long-time group of players who meet twice monthly (some of its members have been meeting for more than twenty years) add all wins to a communal kitty used to fund an annual mah-jongg-playing weekend at the popular coastal resort of Sea Ranch, California. The kitty covers the cost of accommodations and food (the fee for the personal masseuse, however, is not included). The idea of a communal mah-jongg piggy bank has been around for years. In the fascinating and entertaining documentary *Mah Jongg: The Tiles That Bind*, one lifelong player of the game recalls groups of Jewish women in the New York area in the 1930s socking away their weekly winnings in their *pishkas* (communal coin purses). At the end of the year, when enough money had accumulated, they'd strike out with their husbands for Coney Island or into midtown Manhattan to see a show. These yearly outings were major events that made for a great night—the women dressed to the nines—in otherwise hard times.

LEARNING TO PLAY THE AMERICAN WAY

Within the United States, second in popularity to the traditional Chinese game is the game supported by the National Mah Jongg League, often referred to as "American mah-jongg." It has been said that American mah-jongg is a more difficult game to learn. This is due in part to the annual *Official Standard Hands and Rules* card issued by the National Mah Jongg League, which makes for a constantly changing game. Just when you think you have things all figured out, an entirely new set of hands is thrown into the mix. While American mah-jongg is lighter on ritual, superstition, and beliefs about luck than its Chinese cousins, it's heavier when it comes to the number of tiles necessary for play (152 tiles, including flower and joker tiles, as opposed to the 144 tiles used in Chinese versions).

How to Play American Mah-Jongg—Simplified Rules of the National Mah Jongg League

American mah-jongg requires the use of joker and flower tiles (season tiles are also called "flowers" in the American game). Unlike in the Chinese version, the numbers on the flower tiles have no bearing on the game. The American game adds an additional 8 joker tiles to the 144 used to learn the Chinese game, for a total of 152 tiles.

4 red dragons

4 white dragons

4 green dragons

4 north winds

4 east winds

4 west winds

4 south winds

4 flowers (one of each, numbered 1 to 4)

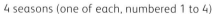

4 seasons (one of each, numbered 1 to 4)

36 craks (four of each number 1 through 9)

36 dots (four of each number 1 through 9)

36 bams (four of each number 1 through 9)

8 jokers

You'll also want to have a copy of the National Mah Jongg League's *Official Standard Hands and Rules* card, and the league's official rule book, *Mah Jongg Made Easy*. (See the Resources section for information on how to acquire these references.)

Game Setup

Step 1: Choosing A Dealer

Unlike in the Chinese version, the first dealer of an American game is usually reserved for the host. If a host is unavailable, each player rolls two dice and the highest roller becomes the first dealer.

Step 2: Shuffling the Tiles and Building the Wall

Racks are typically used in the American game. Each player has a rack in front of her, and the walls are built in front of the rack.

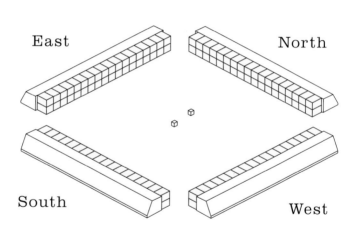

Courtesy

ONLY USE YOUR RIGHT HAND TO DRAW A TILE FROM THE WALL
OR TO RETRIEVE A DISCARDED TILE.

Step 3: Breaking the Wall

The wall is broken the same way as in the Chinese version; however, instead of three dice, only two are being used.

The wall from which tiles are being drawn is pushed forward by the player seated behind it.

Exposed tiles are placed face up, on the top of the rack for other players to see.

Each player's hand sits on the rack, facing the player.

Rules of Play

The object of the American version is the same as that of the Chinese game: to create a winning hand composed of various groupings of tiles. The American version, however, requires that all hands be based on the hands listed in the National Mah Jongg League's *Official Standard Hand and Rules* card. Once you obtain a card, study its instructions regarding how to interpret its symbols and familiarize yourself with those symbols so you can decide which hand to go for during play without holding up the game for others.

Sets or Groups of Tiles

Most of the tile groupings are the same as those in the Chinese version of the game, although the chow (three tiles of the same suit in a sequence) is called a "combination of numerals" and does not require all tiles to be sequential. Other differences include the addition of the quint, the inclusion of joker tiles, and the use of flower tiles.

What's in a Quint?

A *quint* is a five-tile grouping, in which one tile must be a joker.

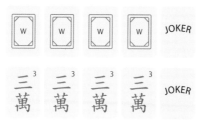

Example: A card may indicate a hand that requires a quint as follows: Four white dragons and a joker or four 3-crak tiles and a joker.

What's in a Combination of Numerals?

A combination of numerals is created from a grouping of three or four-suit tiles in a particular order.

Example: A card may indicate a hand that requires a combination of numerals as follows: a 3-bam, a 6-bam, and a 9-bam.

Distinguishing Features of the American Game
Jokers

Jokers are essentially wild cards and may be used to stand in for any tile (except in a specifically joker-less hand, indicated on the card). Jokers are used in a game in several ways, discussed below.

⊙ DISCARDING A JOKER

During a player's turn, he or she may discard a joker, but the joker must be declared for the rest of the hand the same as the tile that was discarded just before it.

> *Example:* The player before you discards a 4-dot tile. It's now your turn, and after you draw a tile, you wish to discard a joker. The discarded joker is therefore treated as if it were a 4-dot tile.

⊙ SWITCHING A JOKER

During a player's turn, he may switch out a joker from any player's exposed pung, kong, or quint and replace it with the appropriate tile from his or her hand.

> *Example:* The player across from you has an exposed pung made up of two 8-craks and a joker. You have one unwanted 8-crak in your hand and you need a joker. When it becomes your turn, you may take the joker from the player across from you by replacing it with your 8-crak.

However, a regular tile in someone else's pung, kong, or quint cannot be switched out and replaced by a joker.

⊙ LIMITATION

Jokers cannot be used to stand in for a single tile in the formation of a pair.

Flowers

Flowers in the American version differ from their Chinese counterparts. They are treated just like regular tiles and are necessary for completing certain hands on the card, unlike in the Chinese version of play, where they are kept separate from the tiles incorporated into normal play, affecting the game only when it comes time to tally the scores.

Reading the Card

The tri-fold card offers forty or fifty tile combinations that make winning hands as well as instructions on how to read the card, plus a basic over-view of the National Mah Jongg League rules. The card itself is printed in three different colors—red, green, and blue, with each color representing a suit. Below are some hints regarding how to read the card.

NOTE: WHITE DRAGON IS USED AS ZERO "O". IT MAY BE USED WITH ANY SUIT. (CRAKS, BAMS OR DOTS)

This document is protected by copyright laws. It is illegal to reproduce it.

2003   VALUES

NN EEE 2003 WWW SS (Any 2 and 3 Same Suit) . . . . **c 30**
FFFF 2003 333 333 (Any 2 Suits, 2 and 3 Same Suit, Pungs 3 Only) . . . . **x 30**
FF GGGG 2003 RRRR (Any 2 and 3 Same Suit) . . . . **x 30**
FFF NEWS FFF 2003 (Any 2 and 3 Same Suit) . . . . **x 25**

2468

22 44 666 888 DDDD . . . . **x 25**
FF 2222 44 66 8888 (Any 2 Suits) . . . . **x 25**
222 444 6666 8888 (Any 3 Suits) . . . . **x 25**
FF 222 DDD 888 DDD (Any 2 Suits) . . . . **c 30**
2222 4444 6666 88 . . . . **x 25**
22 44 444 666 8888 (Any 3 Suits, Kong 8's Only) . . . . **x 25**
222 44 666 888 888 (Any 3 Suits, Pungs 8's other 2 Suits) . . . . . . **c 35**

LIKE NUMBERS

FF 1111 1111 1111 (Any Like Nos.) . . . . **x 25**
11 DD 111 DDD 1111 (Any Like Nos.) . . . . **c 30**
FFF 1111 FFF 1111 (Any Like Nos.) . . . . **x 25**

QUINTS

FF 11111 66 77777 or **FF 11111 66 77777** (These Nos. Only)
DDDDD FFFF 11111 (Quint Any Dragon and Any No., Any Suit) . . . .
22222 3333 44444 (Any 3 Consecutive Nos., Any 3 Suits). . . . . . .
NNNNN EE WW SSSSS

CONSECUTIVE RUN

11 22 333 444 5555 or **55 66 777 888 9999** . . . . . .
1111 222 3333 DDD (Any 3 Consecutive Nos., Any 2 Suits) . . . . . .
11 22 33 44 5555 or **5555 66 77 88 9999** (Any 2 Suits) .
11 22 111 222 3333 (Any 3 Consecutive Nos., Any 3 Suits) . . . . . .
111 222 3333 4444 (Any 4 Consecutive Nos., Any 3 Suits) . . . . . .
FFFF 1111 2222 DD (Any 2 Consecutive Nos.) . . . .

13579

11 33 555 777 9999 . . . .
111 333 3333 5555 (Any 3 Suits) . . . .
555 777 7777 9999 (Any 3 Suits) . . . .
FF 1111 9999 DDDD (Any 3 Suits) . . . .
11 33 55 7777 9999 (Any 3 Suits) . . . .
FF 1 33 555 1 33 555 (Any 2 Suits) . . . .
FF 5 77 999 5 77 999 (Any 2 Suits) . . . .
FFFF 3333 × 5555 = 15 or **FFFF 5555 × 7777 = 35** . . . .

A single color used to depict a hand signifies that one suit must be used in that hand.

for example: **22 44 666 888 DDDD**

Two colors indicate that the hand must be played in two different suits. Three colors indicate three suits.

for example: **FF 2222 44 66 8888**

The monetary value to be paid for each hand is indicated by the number immediately following the *c* or *x* symbol on the card.

for example: . . .**x 25**

Below are the symbols on the card along with their meanings:

    N: north
    E: east
    W: west
    S: south
    F: flower
    D: dragon
    C: concealed hand
    X: exposed hand

Instructions in parentheses after the listed hand indicate an optional way of playing the hand. If there are no parenthetical instructions following the listed hand, then the hand must be played exactly as illustrated.

for example:

FF GGGG 2003 RRRR (Any 2 and 3 Same Suit)

WINDS – DRAGONS	VALUES
E WWW SSS FFFF	x 25
N 11 11 11 **SSSS** (Pairs Any Like Odd Nos.)	x 30
22 **22** 22 **WWWW** (Pairs Any Like Even Nos.)	x 30
DDDD SSS DDDD (Any 2 Dragons)	x 25
DDD WWW DDDD (Any 2 Dragons)	x 25
N EEEE WWWW SS	x 25

369	
3 66 999 DDDD	x 25
3 66 999 3333 (Any 2 Suits, Kong 3, 6 or 9)	x 25
666 6666 **9999** (Any 3 Suits)	x 25
666 9999 DDD (Any 2 Suits)	x 25
33 6666 9999	x 25
3 33 66 99 **3333** (Any 3 Suits, Kong 3, 6 or 9)	c 30

SINGLES AND PAIRS	
R 33 44 55 66 77 (Any Run 7 Pairs)	c 45
1 33 55 77 99 SS	c 45
22 44 66 88 WW	c 45
34 55 55 678 99 (Any 2 Suits)	c 45
69 DD 3669 DD (Any 2 Suits)	c 50
1223 112233 or 998 99887 998877	c 45
03 NEWS 2003 (1 or 2 Suits, 2 and 3 Same Suit)	c 75

Each suit has a corresponding dragon color:

craks: red
dots: white
bams: green

If a hand is illustrated in one color and numbers and dragons are called for, the suit and dragons must match.

for example: **FFFF 3 66 999 DDDD**

If, on the other hand, the numbers are shown in one color and the dragons in another, then the suit and dragons must *not* match.

for example: **EEE DDDD WWW DDDD**

Hands are listed categorically, which offers players a place to start looking for the type of hand best suited to the tiles they have drawn. Categories may change slightly with any given year, and there may be some overlap from one category to another. The following are some of the categories:

ⓐ The Year (2003 on this card): hands involving the year in which the card is in effect

ⓑ 2468: hands including these particular numbers

ⓒ Like Numbers: hands that are made up of combinations of same numbers or symbols

ⓓ Quint: hands made up of quints

ⓔ Consecutive Run: hands that are made up of consecutive numbers

ⓕ 13579: hands including these particular numbers

ⓖ Winds-Dragons: hands utilizing a combination of winds and/or dragons

ⓗ 369: hands including these particular numbers

ⓘ Singles and Pairs: hands made up of tiles as indicated on the card.

The Charleston

One of the main differences between the Chinese and American games is the exchange of tiles at the start of the game, known as the "Charleston." This provides players a chance to get rid of unwanted tiles right off the bat; however, jokers may never be passed in a Charleston.

Tip: It is best not to pass two or three of a kind, all dragons, all winds, or all the same numeral, lest you aid another player's winning hand.

⊙ THE FIRST CHARLESTON

This maneuver is mandatory, even if a player has drawn a complete winning hand from the wall.

Pass 1: Each player passes three undesired tiles to the person on her right. The players take a look at their newly acquired tiles and select three unwanted tiles for the second pass. The three unwanted tiles selected for the second pass could very well end up being the same tiles just received. Pass 2: Each player passes three undesired tiles to the person opposite her.

Courtesy

DURING PLAY, YOU SHOULD ALWAYS CALL OUT THE TILES YOU DISCARD
SO THAT EVERYONE (ESPECIALLY THOSE BUSY GOSSIPING OR EATING)
CAN FOLLOW THE PLAY.

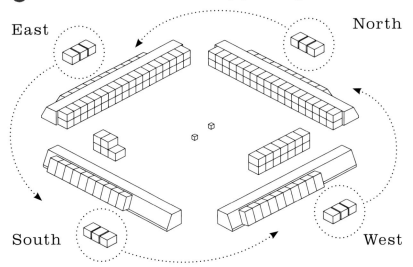

a First Pass: Pass three undesired tiles to the player to the right.

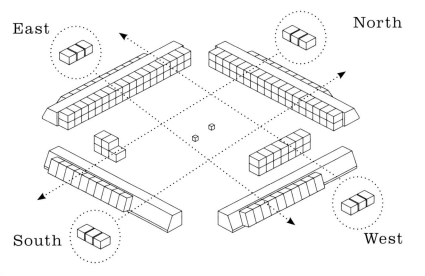

b Second Pass: Pass three undesired tiles to the player seated across.

East North

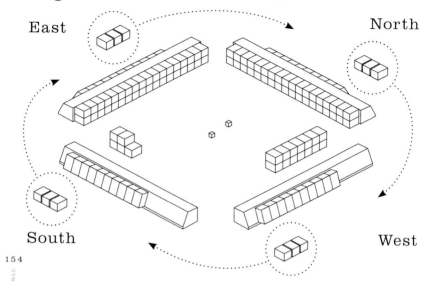

South West

Pass 3: Each player passes three undesired tiles to the person on her left. On this pass only, if someone prefers not to part with any more of her tiles she can opt for a "blind pass," in which she takes one, two, or all three of the tiles that are being passed to her and immediately passes them to the player to her left without looking at them.

⊙ THE SECOND CHARLESTON

This second Charleston is done only if all four players agree to do it. If anyone objects to it, the second Charleston is not initiated.

Pass 1: Three undesired tiles go to the player on the left.
Pass 2: Three undesired tiles go to the player opposite.

Pass 3: Three undesired tiles go to the player on the right. As is the case in the first Charleston, a blind pass can be made at this juncture.

⊙ OPTIONAL PASS

After completing the first and possibly the second Charleston, you have one final option to pass. One, two, or three tiles may be passed to the player in the opposite seat. The number of tiles exchanged is decided by the player wanting the smaller number. If one of the players does not want to exchange any tiles, then no tiles are passed between the two players involved in the potential exchange.

Time to Play

Once the Charleston has been completed, play of the game itself is nearly identical to that of the Chinese game. East, with fourteen tiles to the others' thirteen, is the first to discard a tile face up, naming its symbol aloud. The dealer's turn is then over. Once the dealer discards a tile it can be claimed by the other players, in accordance with the same rules from the Chinese version.

Pungs and kongs (quints are not present in the Chinese game, though in principle they are similar to pungs and kongs) are virtually the same as they are in Chinese mah-jongg. When a player pungs, kongs, or quints, known as "calling" in American mah-jongg, he or she must place the exposed tiles on the rack in front of him or her. The player then discards an unwanted tile, and it becomes the next player's turn (the person seated to the right). Similar to the Chinese version, some players' turns may be skipped as a result of a pung, kong, or quint.

DIM SUM

Dim sum literally means "small hearts" in Chinese. This traditional Chinese cuisine in which small fried or steamed dumplings are served is one of our favorite mah-jongg snacks. Each serving is small (and easy to manage between mah-jongg hands) and does not require to be served hot—perfect for late-night games.

SHRIMP DUMPLING	PORK DUMPLING	SPRING ROLL
(har gau)	(siu mai)	(chun cune)

蝦角	燒賣	春卷

GLUTINOUS RICE DUMPLING
(ham sue kok)

咸水角

BBQ PORK BUN
(xia siu bao)

叉燒包

SESAME BALL
(qin teu)

煎堆

EGG TART
(tan tat)

蛋撻

TURNIP CAKE
(lo bak co)

蘿蔔糕

DEEP-FRIED TARO ROOT WITH MEAT
(wu kok)

芋角

If Nobody Wins

As in Chinese mah-jongg, occasionally nobody wins. When all the tiles have been drawn and no one has declared a winning hand, a wall game is called. Players simply turn the tiles over, mix them thoroughly, and build the four walls again. The person to the right of the original dealer becomes east, the dice are thrown, the wall is broken at the designated place, and tiles are picked. The Charleston is repeated and the game begins as before.

Score!

The *Official Standard Hands and Rules* card makes scoring fairly straightforward in American mah-jongg. However, players need to first decide whether they will play with chips (representing points) or real money.

In the Chips

If you go the chip route, you can use the point values given by the National Mah Jongg League and dole out the following quantities of chips to each player at the start of play:

two chips of the same color to represent 200 points each (400 points)
four chips of the same color to represent 100 points each (400 points)
six chips of the same color to represent 25 points each (150 points)
ten chips of the same color to represent 5 points each (50 points)

These chips represent a total amount of 1,000 points per player given out at the commencement of the game.

The value of each hand is listed under the heading "Values" on the card.

LOVE *or* MONEY

Some players consider it unwise to play for money in games with friends or family members, while others counter that only when there's money involved do people take the game seriously and play their best. Many longtime players will admit that they have no interest in playing if there's no cash on the line and won't even attend a game where betting is not part of the equation. Beginners, however, are encouraged to play for money only in games that have an established limit on losses (a *pie*), which is established at the beginning of the evening's game. This is a friendlier type of play that allows the bankrupt player to continue to play the game; the player may collect from other players if he or she makes a mah-jongg but is not required to pay any more winners until he or she gains back some working capital.

This way, even if a player loses her pie, at least she'll keep her shirt.

A couple of additional rules can affect the distribution of points. First, when a player self-draws a winning hand (meaning he picks his own mah-jongg tile from the wall instead of acquiring it through another player's discard), all players pay that player double the value of the hand.

> *Example:* If the winning hand is valued at 35 points, then each player must then pay the winner 70 points.

Second, when a player mah-jonggs as a result of another player's discard, then only the discarder is required to pay double while all other players pay the hand's stated value. At the end of a game of mah-jongg, groups of players may convert these chips into actual money.

In the American game, when a player mah-jonggs and his hand does not contain a joker, all players pay the winner double the value of the hand.

SCORE CARDS, CIRCA 1923

In the Money

If you choose to play with money in order to add excitement to the game, simply substitute monetary denominations for the point values listed on the card (for example, 1 point might equal one cent). Most players just pay the amount indicated on the card under "Values," which may range from 25 to 75 points (cents). In order to limit losses, before playing many groups will establish a pie, or the maximum amount that can be lost in any given game.

MAH-JONGG GAME STRATEGY FOR ALL VERSIONS

Winning mah-jongg is not only the result of luck. As they gain experience, mah-jongg players learn to use strategies to improve their chances of winning. One defensive strategy, called "dogging a hand," involves discarding tiles that are of no use to the other players, even if doing so depletes the discarder's hand. As one defensive player says, "I'd rather ruin my own hand any day of the week than see someone else win and me have to pay." As the National Mah Jongg League's official handbook, *Mah Jongg Made Easy*, states, "You cannot Mah Jongg second."

Another strategic approach found in the American style of play is based on intimidation: playing without the National Mah Jongg League card in front of you. This tactic is a signal to others that you have memorized the hands and are not to be messed with. In a similar vein, a kind of Darwinian situation can sometimes occur among players of the American version at the beginning of the year when the new card has just been issued and players are grappling with it for the first time. In these cases, slower learners are occasionally criticized by their quick-study counterparts for holding up the game, and may be encouraged (sometimes without much tact) to study the card on their own stinking time. It is not uncommon for players who have faced this kind of peer pressure to go home and practice the game alone, frenetically occupying all the seating positions themselves. It may sound a bit like trying to play musical chairs solo, but it *is* a good way to get in some practice using the new card and avoid further public humiliation.

CHILDREN'S MAH-JONGG BOX COVER, CIRCA 1920

Whichever variation or style you choose to play, understand that mah-jongg is a game that you absorb over time. As with chess, which is learned gradually, you can best learn mah-jongg by playing, talking to others, reading books, and researching hands and scoring procedures online. Rome wasn't built in a day, and mah-jongg wasn't learned in one, either. Enjoy the journey!

HAND-CARVED BAMBOO AND BONE MAH-JONGG TILES, CIRCA 1923

RESOURCES

GENERAL INFORMATION

www.mahjongmuseum.com

Jim May's Mah Jong Cyber Museum offers historical information and photos, along with a large private collection of tile sets and related items, and links to other helpful sites.

www.sloperama.com

Tom Sloper's well-organized site covers all the mah-jongg bases, offering personal responses to submitted questions, answers to frequently asked queries, mah-jongg exchange boards, and links to newsgroups, domestic and international tournaments, and teachers.

ORGANIZATIONS

National Mah Jongg League

250 West 57th Street

New York, NY 10107

Phone: (212) 246-3052

Fax: (212) 246-4117

www.nationalmahjonggleague.org

The NMJL publishes the rule booklet *Mah Jongg Made Easy*, as well as the annual *Official Standard Hands and Rules* card. The league also sells merchandise (including mah-jongg playing cards), replaces missing mah-jongg playing pieces, answers questions and arbitrates disputes about individual games, officiates National Mah Jongg League Internet games, and sponsors tournaments and mah-jongg cruises.

American Mah-Jongg Association

8605 Snowreath Road

Baltimore, MD 21208

Toll-free: (800) 663-4581

Local: (410) 580-1357

Fax: (410) 580-1358

E-mail: amermja@aol.com

www.amja.net

Like the NMJA, the AMJA also issues an annual card, offers merchandise such as yakitori markers, and facilitates tournaments and cruises. Membership perks include a quarterly newsletter and use of a toll-free number for help with mah-jongg questions and assistance with locating other interested players in your area.

Wright-Patterson Officers' Wives' Club

Mah-Jongg Book Sales

P.O. Box 1067

Fairborn, OH 45324

www.wrightpattersonowc.org/mahjongg.html

For those who wish to adopt the game established and played by officers' wives on American military bases worldwide, the club offers rule books for sale.

TOURNAMENTS AND CRUISES

Travel Wizard

7788 University Avenue

La Mesa, CA 91941

Toll-free: 800-708-7677

Local: (619) 464-1946

Fax: (619) 462-5278

www.travelwizardtravel.com

Travel Wizard organizes both land and sea tournaments, most notably the Cruise, Schmooze, and Mahj competitions aboard ships with destinations to Mexico, Alaska, Hawaii, the Caribbean, Canada, New England, Europe, and the Panama Canal.

Mah-Jongg Madness (now Specialty Cruises International)

677 N. Washington Blvd, #80

Sarasota, FL 34236-4241

Toll-free: (866) MAH-JONG

Fax: (941) 379-8097

www.mahjongg.org

Mah-Jongg Madness hosts land tournaments in cities dotting the East Coast, the Midwest, and Florida in addition to an annual weeklong Caribbean tournament-at-sea cruise for the National Mah Jongg League.

www.mahjongnews.com

This site offers information regarding tournaments held in Europe and Asia.

MAH-JONGG-RELATED PRODUCTS

Garage sales, auctions, flea markets, antique stores, and Chinatowns the world over are all great places to find both antique and modern sets, as are many Internet sites. Most of the official mah-jongg organizations listed previously sell sets on their sites or at least provide recommended links. The following sites are additional good sources of new and old sets and paraphernalia:

www.ebay.com

eBay is a great source for antique sets, tables, jewelry, and other mah-jongg merchandise.

www.mahjonggmaven.com

This site offers modern sets and other mah-jongg-related items for sale. It also provides the opportunity to design your own set, from case to shape and color of tiles.

www.windfallrepublic.com

Windfall Republic sells artful hand-carved sets direct from China.

Replacement and Custom Tiles

www.arkayengravers.com/tiles/

Personalized tiles sold on this site and others like it can feature every-thing from words and symbols to the faces of friends, relatives, or pets.

Tables

In Asia, where tile racks are not customary, players use special mah-jongg tables with a felt top and built-in lip to keep the tiles from falling off during play. These sorts of tables are equipped with cup holders, small drawers, and ashtrays. Some tables made in Japan and China are even more elaborate, with mechanized features. For tables and related items, check out the following Web sites:

www.jollyoptics.com/mjtable.html

www.rakuten.co.jp/kasiken/

This Japanese-language site gives its prices in yen.

www.wherethewindsblow.com

This site offers custom-designed felt table covers, in addition to soaps and teddy bears decorated with mah-jongg symbols.

JEWELRY AND TCHOTCHKES

There is no shortage of ways devotees of the game have managed to weave tiles into adornments, from the wacky to the chic.

www.medicimint.com

This site sells white, dark, and milk chocolate tiles housed in gift boxes modeled after antique Chinese mah-jongg set carrying cases.

www.kmainindustries.com

Gifts of all kinds, including tile-shaped candles, are sold by this company.

www.borninmommysheart.com

This company sells beautiful bracelets made from mah-jongg tiles.

www.esdeeandbyhishand.com

This site is a good source for mah-jongg earrings, necklaces, pendants, and some very pretty bracelets.

www.tias.com/stores/eclecticelementstwo/

Eclectic Elements Two, which describes itself as "chunky, funky, rockabilly, and retro," has a great selection of mah-jongg jewelry in a wide array of materials, including Bakelite and catalin.

FURTHER READING, FURTHER VIEWING

Mah-Jongg: The Tiles That Bind is a BTG Productions documentary by Bari Pearlman and Phyllis Heller exploring the shared experiences of Asian American and Jewish American women as they play the game and make it a part of their lives. The film is available for purchase at: *www.mahjonggmovie.com*.

Mah-Jongg as Fortune Teller

For more information about the ancient Chinese practice of telling fortunes by reading mah-jongg tiles the following two books by Derek Walters are a good place to start: *Fortune-telling by Mah Jongg: A Practical Guide to Divination Using the Ancient Chinese Game of Mah Jongg* and *The Fortune Teller's Mah Jongg: The Ancient Game as a Modern Oracle*.

Bakelite

To learn more about Bakelite, read the authoritative article by Lloyd and Stephen Fadem on the Web site of the magazine *Deco Echoes*: *www.deco-echoes.com/bakelite.html*

ACKNOWLEDGMENTS

We'd like to thank the many people who helped us bring this book into being: first, the able staff at Chronicle Books, including editor Steve Mockus, whose talent, guidance, and encouragement have been worth more than their weight in martinis; associate publisher Debra Lande, for her grace and generosity; design coordinator Jacob Gardner; copyeditor Karen O'Donnell Stein; associate managing editor Jan Hughes; senior production coordinator Tera Killip; and publicity director Andrea Burnett (and her mother, Lee, for her kugel recipe).

We want to express our appreciation to David Chau, Mark Liu, Albert So, Belinda Yin, and Jennifer Ma, who so patiently answered our daily questions about mah-jongg rules and strategies, and to Debra Lande, Roz Joseph, Gail Friedlander, Jennifer Nichols, Toby Salk, Susan Giba, Sharon Gillenwater, and Clara Chun for allowing us to be a fly on the wall with a notepad during your games.

We extend special thanks to Jason Mitchell and Chris Palumbo and his family for providing a rejuvenating writer's retreat in Connecticut. We are immensely grateful to the following people for their contributions and their time: National Mah Jongg-League president Ruth Unger, Roberta and Steve Last of Travel Wizard, Dorothy and Larry Krams of Mah Jongg Madness, Dorothy Kornheiser, Jane Horn, Kristian Jansen Jaech of Windfall Republic, Bari Pearlman of BTG Productions, and Sandra Davis of Esdee.

Thanks are due to Jim May for sharing his mah-jongg-related treasures as well as their images.

We thank Tom Sloper for enlightening us about the world of mah-jongg, and Kelly Powers, for capturing the beauty of mah-jongg with her lens, all while balancing on a broken leg.

ABOUT THE AUTHORS